Build Your Shy Kid's Self-Confidence

Give Them the Foundation to Overcome Anxiety to Thrive in Life, Relationships, and Opportunities

Lucy Quentin

© Copyright 2023 - All rights reserved.

The content contained within this book may not be reproduced, duplicated or transmitted without direct written permission from the author or the publisher.

Under no circumstances will any blame or legal responsibility be held against the publisher, or author, for any damages, reparation, or monetary loss due to the information contained within this book, either directly or indirectly.

Legal Notice:

This book is copyright protected. It is only for personal use. You cannot amend, distribute, sell, use, quote or paraphrase any part, or the content within this book, without the consent of the author or publisher.

Disclaimer Notice:

Please note the information contained within this document is for educational and entertainment purposes only. All effort has been executed to present accurate, up to date, reliable, complete information. No warranties of any kind are declared or implied. Readers acknowledge that the author is not engaged in the rendering of legal, financial, medical or professional advice. The content within this book has been derived from various sources. Please consult a licensed professional before attempting any techniques outlined in this book.

By reading this document, the reader agrees that under no circumstances is the author responsible for any losses, direct or indirect, that are incurred as a result of the use of the information contained within this document, including, but not limited to, errors, omissions, or inaccuracies.

Table of Contents

INTRODUCTION 1

CHAPTER 1: UNDERSTANDING SHYNESS AND LACK OF SOCIAL CONFIDENCE 3

DEFINING SHYNESS AND INTROVERSION 4
   Shyness 4
   Introversion 4
WHY SHYNESS HAPPENS 6
   Feelings in the Brain 6
   Thought Habits 7
   Unintentional Body Language 7
   Skills That Need Practice 7
   The Tough Social World 7
THE SPECTRUM OF SHYNESS 9
DEBUNKING MYTHS ABOUT SHYNESS 10
   Myth #1: Shyness Is Just a Phase. They'll Grow Out of It. 10
   Myth #2: Shy Kids Need to Be "Fixed" or Forced Out of Their Shells. 10
   Myth #3: Shy Kids Will Struggle Academically. 11
   Myth #4: Shy Kids Don't Want to Make Friends. 11
   Myth #5: Shyness Is Something Kids Can Easily Control. 11
CASE STUDY: SARAH 11
CASE STUDY: JAKE 12
WRAPPING UP 14

CHAPTER 2: WHY CONFIDENCE IS IMPORTANT AND HOW IT MAY IMPACT A CHILD'S DEVELOPMENT AND PROGRESS 15

SOCIAL AND EMOTIONAL IMPORTANCE 16
WHY SPEAKING UP MATTERS 17
   Brain Growth Needs Use 17
   Feedback Shapes Identity 17
   New Coping Strategies Emerge 18
   Overall Wellness Suffers 18
WHY CONFIDENCE MATTERS 18
   Shapes Friendships 19
   Grows the Brain 19
   Boosts Coping Abilities 19
   Supports Learning 19
ACADEMIC RELEVANCE 20

IMPENDING ADOLESCENCE...21
CASE STUDY: MICHAEL..23
CASE STUDY: SOPHIA..24
OPPORTUNITIES ABOUND 25

CHAPTER 3: RECOGNIZING THE SIGNS IN YOUR CHILD......27

HOW TO RECOGNIZE THAT A CHILD IS SHY AND LACKING IN SOCIAL
CONFIDENCE 27
WHERE DOES PERSONALITY FIT INTO SHYNESS? 29
  *Distinction Between Shyness and Lack of Social Confidence With
  Social Anxiety..30*
THE TIME TO ASK FOR PROFESSIONAL HELP 32
CASE STUDY: ALEX 33
CASE STUDY: EMMA 34
OBSERVATIONAL AWARENESS...35

CHAPTER 4: CREATING A SUPPORTIVE AND ENCOURAGING ENVIRONMENT 37

TEACHING ASSERTIVENESS AND SELF-CONFIDENCE 37
ENCOURAGING ACTIVITIES, INTERESTS, AND HOBBIES 39
  Nurturing Growth 40
  Helping Develop and Encourage a Growth Mindset......................41
THE CRUCIAL ROLE OF SCHOOLS 42
  Setting the Tone...42
  Curriculum Considerations 43
  Peers Can Help 43
  Leverage Staff 43
  Partner Proactively...43
  Adjust Expectations, Not the Child...44
CASE STUDY: LIAM 44
CASE STUDY: ELLA 45
ENVIRONMENT MATTERS 46

CHAPTER 5: STRATEGIES FOR HELPING YOUR CHILD NAVIGATE SOCIAL SITUATIONS 49

CHOOSING THE RIGHT SCHOOL AND EDUCATIONAL ENVIRONMENT............49
ENCOURAGING INVOLVEMENT IN ACTIVITIES, HOBBIES, AND NEW
EXPERIENCES 51
ORGANIZED PLAYDATES AND ACTIVITIES..53
THE PIVOTAL ROLE OF PARENTS 54
  Demonstrate Speaking Up 55
  Talk Through Social Struggles 55
  Applaud Small Daily Wins..55
  Structure Optimal Conditions..56
  Redirect Critical Messages..56
  Collaborate on Coping Skills...56
  Explore Social Stories...57

Consider Counseling 57
CASE STUDY: NOAH 57
CASE STUDY: LILY 58
SECURE AND CONNECTED 59

CHAPTER 6: SPECIFIC COMMUNICATION STRATEGIES TO HELP YOUR CHILD 61

BREAKING THE ICE 61
DEVELOPING FRIENDSHIPS 63
BEING A GOOD FRIEND 64
MANAGING SOCIAL ANXIETY 65
PARENT-TEACHER COLLABORATION 66
   Observe Global Functioning 67
   Compare Observations 67
   Strategize Gradual Steps 67
   Emphasize Assets 68
   Coordinate Touchpoints 68
CASE STUDY: SAM 68
CASE STUDY: CLARA 69
NURTURED COMMUNICATION 70

CHAPTER 7: WHAT ARE THE IMPLICATIONS FOR YOUR SHY CHILD AT SCHOOL? 73

BUILDING THE RIGHT RELATIONSHIPS AND PARTNERSHIPS WITH SCHOOL TEACHERS AND OTHER STAFF 74
SPEAKING UP AND ADVOCATING YOUR CHILD'S NEEDS AT SCHOOL 75
HAVING ALIGNMENT AND AGREEMENT ON THE STRATEGIES TO HELP YOUR CHILD AT SCHOOL AND HOME 77
ENCOURAGING SOCIAL ENGAGEMENTS AND ACTIVITIES AT SCHOOL 79
GIVING SHY KIDS OPPORTUNITIES TO LEAD 81
HOW SCHOOLS CAN ENCOURAGE SHY KIDS 82
   Give Advance Notice 82
   Highlight Their Skills 82
   Allow Breaks 82
   Match Buddies 83
   Applaud All Progress 83
   Make Participation Options 83
   Involve Families 83
CASE STUDY: MAY 84
CASE STUDY: ADA 84
OPPORTUNITIES ABOUND 85

CHAPTER 8: HOW TECHNOLOGY, DIGITIZATION, AND SOCIAL MEDIA IS IMPACTING SHY CHILDREN 87

THE IMPACT OF TECHNOLOGY ON SOCIAL DEVELOPMENT 87
MONITORING ONLINE INTERACTIONS 89

Setting Screen Time Limits (and the Tough Conversations That Go Along With It) 90
Digital Etiquette and Safety 91
Promoting Healthy Gaming for Shy Kids 93
Promoting Healthy Social Media Habits 96
   Discuss Online Identity Mindfully 96
   Set Private Accounts 97
   Encourage Bond-Building Platforms 97
   Monitor Balance 97
   Address Online Drama Compassionately 98
   Coach Confident Self-Expression 98
Case Study: Grace 99
The Next Generation 99

CHAPTER 9: CULTIVATING QUIET SUPERPOWERS 101

Empathy and Emotional Intelligence 101
Creativity and Innovation 102
Quiet Leadership Strengths 103
Resilience and Mental Toughness 104
Self-Aware Identities 104
Leveraging Sensitivity as a Leadership Strength 105
   Noticing Unmet Needs 105
   Leading Through Listening 105
   Persisting Toward Purpose 105
   Centering Ethics and Inclusion 106
   Supporting Behind the Scenes 106
Case Study: Rico 106
Case Study: Nora 107
Gifts Abound 108

CHAPTER 10: CHALLENGES AND HOW TO MANAGE THEM 111

Setbacks Are Part of the Process 111
Role of Resilience 113
   Harnessing the Power of "Yet" 113
   Replenishing Your Resilience 114
Problem-Solving and Coping Strategies 115
When to Ask for Professional Help 116
The Power of Peer Support Networks 117
Cultivating Confidence Through Interests 118
   Discover Innate Fascinations 118
   Help Broaden Exposure 119
   Encourage Skill Development 119
   Facilitate Idea Expression 119
   Find Community Belonging 120
   Spotlight Success 120
Case Study: Evan 120
Case Study: Anna 121

OPPORTUNITIES FOR PRACTICE 122
CONCLUSION 125
REFERENCES 127
A NOTE FROM THE AUTHOR 129

Introduction

As parents, we want our children to grow into happy, confident, and kind human beings. We envisage them making friends easily, speaking up for themselves, and embracing new opportunities and challenges with optimism. For some children, their innate shyness makes easy social interaction a real struggle. Shyness is not simply behavioral but has roots in one's temperament and personality right from childhood. While shyness will look different in every child, the underlying challenges remain the same.

For the parents of shy or introverted children, this vision can feel out of reach. You watch your child hesitate to join groups on the playground, stay silent when called upon by a teacher, or avoid initiating play dates. Your heart breaks when they get left out of social events or sit alone during every school break. Their reluctance and avoidance of social situations are confusing when you know they are creative, kind, and interesting kids inside. Despite your best efforts to encourage and support them, their shyness persists. You can't force them out of their shell overnight, yet you still worry about the implications if they don't develop the confidence to learn to navigate social situations. Will they fall behind academically? Struggle to make friends? Develop anxiety or depression? The worry can keep you up at night.

As the parent of a shy child myself, I understand this constant concern. I would do anything to build my daughter's confidence so she can thrive both socially and emotionally. Seeing her struggle day after day and not being able to fix it is heartbreaking for any parent. That situation led me to extensively research and seek professional advice about childhood shyness. What I've learned is that while shy kids face some unique challenges, there is a lot we as parents can do to set them up for social success and grow in confidence. With some concerted effort, shy kids can develop social skills and confidence.

In this book, I want to share the insights and strategies I've gathered over years of trial and error with my own shy child. My goal is to help you, as the parent or caregiver of a shy or introverted child, to:

- understand the psychology behind shyness and where your child falls on the spectrum of average variation.
- recognize the signs that indicate support needed versus typical introverted tendencies.
- create an encouraging environment that builds confidence from a young age.
- apply specific communication and social skill-building techniques.
- partner effectively with your child's school.
- navigate the impact of technology and social media.
- manage ongoing challenges and recognize when professional help may be needed.

With some guidance, you can learn to advocate for your child, bolster their confidence, and set them up to thrive both socially and emotionally.

With the right support, shy children can blossom socially and emotionally, making friendships that bolster their confidence. Every child deserves to feel confident and socially fulfilled regardless of their innate shyness. This book will walk you through making that vision a reality for your special shy child.

Chapter 1:

Understanding Shyness and Lack of Social Confidence

Many of us will inevitably encounter a shy child, whether they're our own or children in our community. Shyness has some biological origins and manifests across a broad spectrum, from mild social hesitation to severe distress interfering with life functioning (Asendorpf, 2008). Approximately 15–50% of children display some degree of shyness (Crozier, 2014), meaning shy kids are far from a unique case. We must deepen our understanding of shyness to nurture these children compassionately.

In this chapter, we will clearly define shyness and introversion, explore various manifestations along the shyness spectrum, debunk common myths that prevent progress, and provide helpful examples and case studies. We'll also incorporate research on the physiology and neurobiology underlying shyness for deeper insight. Our goal is to gain a nuanced working knowledge of shyness to enable us to tailor our support strategies appropriately in subsequent chapters. Embracing and understanding some of the truths about shyness sets the stage for emotional growth.

As parents, we can easily misinterpret our shy child's reluctance to interact socially. We may minimize their discomfort, assume it's temporary, or try forcing them out of their shell. But shy kids face real emotional hurdles that demand sensitivity and support.

The first step lies in truly understanding shyness, how it manifests, and what drives it developmentally. Only with proper understanding can we discern variations in temperament from problematic anxiety requiring intervention. We also must challenge common myths about shy kids so we can empathize with their struggles.

Arming ourselves with knowledge of the issue sets us up to make shy kids feel understood. Only then can we implement the most effective support strategies, which we'll cover in subsequent chapters. Knowledge precedes meaningful help. Let's start building our understanding.

Defining Shyness and Introversion

Before diving into helping our shy kids, it's important to clearly define what we mean by shyness and how it differs from introversion. Shyness and introversion are often used interchangeably but have distinct meanings. Understanding the difference is crucial for supporting shy children appropriately.

Shyness

Shyness refers to feeling uncomfortable, nervous, or inhibited in social situations, especially with unfamiliar people. Shy children may have difficulty initiating conversations, joining groups, maintaining eye contact, or speaking up even when they want to. They often feel self-conscious and worried about how they are perceived by others. This discomfort frequently stems from a lack of confidence rather than a lack of desire to interact. With patience and encouragement, shy kids can learn to navigate social situations.

Introversion

Introversion, on the other hand, simply means someone derives energy from quiet, minimally stimulating environments. Introverts can certainly be shy, but introversion itself defines how someone gets their energy. Many introverts have good social skills even if they opt to spend less time in highly social situations. Introverts choose solitary activities to recharge, while shyness results from anxiety in social situations.

Importantly, shyness differs physiologically from introversion. Research shows shyness correlates with heightened sensitivity and activation in brain regions governing fear and threat response, including the amygdala (Clauss et al., 2014). The amygdala is a small, almond-shaped structure deep in the brain that helps control emotions and motivation. It's basically the brain's emotional control center. The amygdala has two major jobs:

- It processes emotional reactions. When you experience an emotionally charged event, the amygdala activates and triggers emotional responses like fear, anger, pleasure, etc. It's the reason you have gut emotional reactions to certain situations.

- It links emotions to memory. The amygdala attaches emotional significance to events and experiences. This makes you more likely to remember things that had a strong emotional impact.

The amygdala is responsible for processing emotional stimuli, triggering emotional reactionalls, and attaching emotions to memories. It helps explain many human behaviors and responses that are driven by emotions rather than logic.

The amygdala provides the emotional spice and color to our experiences and memories. Without an amygdala, a person may have limited emotions and trouble forming strong memories. Introversion stems more from variations in arousal regulation brain networks. What this means is that shy children may perceive social uncertainty as frightening, not merely uninteresting.

The key difference lies in comfort levels. Introverts choose to avoid social stimulation when they need to recharge. Shy people want to connect but feel unable to or are held back by fear and anxiety. As we've learned, shyness largely stems from a lack of confidence rather than a lack of desire to interact. Recognizing this core distinction guides us in supporting our shy or introverted kids.

Genes also play a substantial role. Twin studies reveal genetics account for 50–60% of dispositional shyness (LoParo & Waldman, 2014). Environment matters, too; but biology establishes clear predispositions. Knowledge of genetic influences helps us separate external pressures that worsen shyness unnecessarily. Kids may not manifest genetically influenced shyness until confronting new situations that trigger innate biology. Awareness of built-in biases guides our approach.

We must understand this distinction so we can better support our shy kids. We need to recognize that they require different coping strategies to minimize social anxiety and build communication skills. Our introverted kids, on the other hand, likely need less intervention, as they simply need quiet time to revive. Defining where your child falls on the shyness spectrum guides you in getting them the right support. Tailoring your responses to address their specific needs makes all the difference.

Why Shyness Happens

When kids are shy, it's not because of bad parenting or something the child is doing wrong. Shyness has many complicated causes working together—some are in the brain and genes, some from how thoughts work, some from lack of practice, and some from how difficult and unpredictable making friends can be. Getting the full picture helps us be patient.

Feelings in the Brain

Parts of shy kids' brains light up strong with fear and worry in social situations even when others see none. It's like their brain shouts "Danger!" when most brains stay quiet. This super-sensitivity is built-in from birth and involves important emotion centers such as the amygdala. It makes new people and risks feel scarier. Understanding this helps us understand why shy kids avoid certain situations. It's not defiance; their brain alarms flood them with messages to flee.

Thought Habits

Shy minds also automatically focus more on noticing frowns or people looking away, ignoring smiles and laughs. They get tunnel vision for problems. They also put themselves down more when left out instead of blaming circumstances. It becomes easy to feel bad. These thought habits grow like weeds from early tough experiences. Seeing thought patterns clearly points us to where help is needed in the mind.

Unintentional Body Language

When overwhelmed, shy bodies often also act nervous without realizing it, fidgeting, looking away, and staying silent even if words are there. Others may take it as rudeness. Simply being aware of this helps both adults and kids since it's not intentional. The body ramps up the pressure.

Skills That Need Practice

Trouble knowing how to join groups, start conversations, keep conversations going, and make eye contact happen because quiet shy kids don't get as much rehearsal. It snowballs. They need more coached play and support, not criticism. Understanding this helps us nurture missing abilities with compassion, not shame. It's about support.

The Tough Social World

Making friends is amazingly complicated! Even for chatty kids, it's tricky. For sensitive kids overwhelmed by noisy large groups who already have had some uncomfortable social situations, it can bring up painful social memories, and it can feel terrifying. Their challenge is greater. If we appreciate how hard managing all the people, actions, jokes, and drama really is, we can see why shy kids cry uncle, retreat within themselves, or walk away.

With care to use simple, kind explanations of everything that makes shyness worse, both kids and parents can team up to make things better step by step with the real causes in mind, not myths about shyness being easy to "outgrow." The problems are real but also solvable.

Beyond the brain, thoughts, skills gaps, and social challenges, there are other key reasons why kids struggle. Some children have more sensitive temperaments from birth, feeling emotions strongly and acutely. Parenting style is hugely impactful too. Critical, impatient, or overprotective parenting often unintentionally compounds shyness instead of soothing it. Cultural expectations around assertiveness also influence how much shyness gets attention and intervention versus acceptance.

Shy kids themselves frequently grapple with self-consciousness, perfectionism, and self-criticism which throttle social confidence, as they meticulously monitor the impressions they think they're making on others. Inner verbal critiques flood their minds, highlighting awkward moments being stored for later worrying. On top of genetics and temperament, parenting and culture, shy kids' inner critics can be their own worst enemy.

Environmental factors also constrain or aid shy kids. Schools short on recess and free play cut critical social practice time. Meanwhile, friendlier schools explicitly teaching social skills can fill competency gaps with compassion. Wider parenting networks sharing rides and coordinating inclusive playdates also help shy recluses incrementally expand their social orbits in manageable steps. Modern tech, despite connecting kids online, may also increase isolation with less in-person practice managing interpersonal nuance and building resilience when facing discomfort. Understanding the wide range of determinants causing shy kids to flounder socially creates a broader menu for gently helping them come out of their shells.

The Spectrum of Shyness

Shyness exists on a broad spectrum, ranging from mild social awkwardness to debilitating social anxiety. Many children fall somewhere in the middle—displaying some shy tendencies in certain situations but otherwise developing age-appropriate social skills. Careful observation helps us identify where our child falls on this spectrum of shyness.

Mild shyness is very common in childhood. Up to 50% of kids seem shy in some contexts, especially around unfamiliar people (Crozier, 2014). This mild shyness typically dissipates with age and experience. These kids likely need little intervention beyond encouragement and opportunities to practice social skills. With maturity, mild shyness usually recedes.

At the other extreme lies social anxiety disorder. About 7–10% of children have true anxiety-related shyness severe enough to interfere with school, activities, and relationships (Crozier, 2014). This excessive shyness accompanied by extreme distress requires treatment from a children's mental health professional. Counseling, therapy, or medication may help in extreme cases.

In between is what we might call "situational shyness." About 15–20% of kids feel shy or uneasy in specific scenarios, such as meeting new people, speaking to authority figures, or in performance situations (Asendorpf, 2008). These kids benefit from slowly expanding their comfort zones and building social confidence. Gradually introducing new social situations allows them to become less hesitant.

Confirming where your child falls on the shyness spectrum relies partly on careful observation over time. Tracking distress and avoidance patterns across different situations paints a more reliable picture. Rating scales like the SAS-A (Social Anxiety Scale for Adolescents) also quantitatively assess shyness levels when unsure (La Greca, 1998). If scores seem concerning, consultation with a child psychologist can help determine appropriate interventions. Keeping detailed records helps discern true severity.

The key is observing where on the shyness spectrum your child lands.

- Mild shyness can be left alone or gently coaxed.
- Situational shyness calls for patient and compassionate support.
- Extreme, distressing shyness requires professional treatment.

As we help our shy kids, we first need to recognize normal variations in temperament so we can tailor our responses appropriately. Adjusting our approach to their degree of shyness makes a big difference.

Debunking Myths About Shyness

Unfortunately, many myths and misconceptions still surround childhood shyness. As parents or caregivers, we need to challenge these myths so we can better empathize with and support our kids. False perceptions only hamper progress.

Myth #1: Shyness Is Just a Phase. They'll Grow Out of It.

Reality: Shyness results from temperament and isn't likely to disappear on its own. Some support through gradual exposure to social situations is often needed. Shyness is innate to one's personality and persists without intervention.

Myth #2: Shy Kids Need to Be "Fixed" or Forced Out of Their Shells.

Reality: Forcing shy kids into uncomfortable situations can further damage their confidence. Gentle encouragement is better, letting their socialization occur at their own pace. Forced interactions generally increase anxiety unnecessarily.

Myth #3: Shy Kids Will Struggle Academically.

Reality: Many shy kids thrive intellectually. Quiet environments can provide better learning settings. Struggles result more from anxiety than academic incompetence. Shyness rarely correlates with intellectual ability (Eggum et al., 2011).

Myth #4: Shy Kids Don't Want to Make Friends.

Reality: Shy kids often desperately want friendships but lack the confidence and skills to initiate. Teaching social strategies can help shy kids connect. Social desire exists but anxiety inhibits action.

Myth #5: Shyness Is Something Kids Can Easily Control.

Reality: Biology and genetics contribute greatly to shyness. Kids cannot simply "get over it" just by deciding to. Patience, empathy, and support are crucial. Shyness does have biological underpinnings.

The reality of childhood shyness is nuanced but absolutely manageable. By abandoning simplistic myths, we can better help our valued shy kids navigate social situations with sensitivity and care. Every child deserves to feel socially fulfilled regardless of innate shyness, and it's our job as parents to nurture their confidence. With truth, empathy, and support, shy kids can thrive.

Case Study: Sarah

Sarah is a quiet 8-year-old who has never had an easy time making friends. At school, she hovers at the edge of groups, hesitates to share her imaginative ideas, and dreads being called on by the teacher, often stumbling over her words. She had one main friend in second grade but was pushed to the side when that friend made new friends.

Playdates require careful planning so Sarah has time to warm up. But, inevitably, when a new child joins, Sarah withdraws to read a book alone instead. Her mom worries about Sarah feeling lonely. She seems to want friends but struggles to speak up assertively.

Sarah shows signs of shyness, feeling uncomfortable and hesitant in unpredictable social situations. This differs from introversion, which relates more to gaining energy from less stimulation. Sarah desperately wants relationships, but anxiety takes over.

Her shyness seems to be situational. She excels in presenting to a familiar class but shuts down among new peers or adults. She likely needs support expanding her comfort zones slowly versus treatment for social anxiety disorder.

Still, her mom worried Sarah's shyness might be something to "grow out of." She's realized shyness results from Sarah's temperament and is unlikely to fade entirely without social skills coaching to increase her confidence. Her daughter needs compassion, not pressure to change.

Armed with a more accurate understanding of shyness, Sarah's parents now better recognize their daughter's challenges. They've stopped believing the myth that Sarah can easily control her shyness. Instead, they sensitively encourage Sarah to incrementally expand her social courage.

Sarah's teacher helps facilitate classroom interactions to support her, too. Her parents also plan to enroll her in a small peer social skills group. With the right assistance tailored to her needs, Sarah's verbal confidence and friendships have begun slowly blossoming.

Case Study: Jake

Jake is a quiet 9-year-old who prefers solo activities like reading, building Lego, and drawing elaborate mazes to playing loud group games on the playground. He has two close friends in his class whom he collaborates with often on projects and sits with at lunch. Jake dislikes noisy, big gatherings like school assemblies and avoids initiating interactions with most classmates.

While somewhat shy, Jake doesn't seem to experience extreme distress in social situations. He maintains eye contact when conversing one-on-one and can order food confidently in restaurants or ask store clerks for help when shopping with his parents. He will also eagerly attend programming classes and interactive museum visits discussing shared interests with peers met during visits.

However, unfamiliar social situations like parties or summer camps have always felt uncomfortable for Jake. Given time to warm up while observing other kids, he participates but avoids leading activities, sticking to peers he knows. Sudden schedule changes or transitioning to new environments provokes visible anxiety interfering with engagement, so he often opts out by claiming boredom or fatigue.

Jake's parents sought guidance from his pediatrician when he began hiding visible nervousness. She explained that Jake shows signs of situational shyness, feeling uncertain about entering new social contexts until he feels safely acclimated. Jake likely needs support continuing to expand his comfort zone combined with coping strategies when he feels overwhelmed. She reassured them that Jake did not meet the criteria for social anxiety disorder, given he maintained close friendships, participated actively when comfortable, and showed no signs of associated depression or refusal to attend school.

Armed with a more nuanced understanding of where Jake's shyness falls on the spectrum, his parents feel equipped to encourage small steps forward socially while respecting his sensitive personality and pace. They plan to enroll him in a summer transition program to help him warm up to unfamiliar environments in anticipation of new classroom peers next year. Jake feels relieved that his natural introversion was explained as a difference, not a deficiency, so he need not feel pressure to become loud and talkative just for the sake of it.

Wrapping Up

Shyness manifests in children across a broad spectrum. By defining shyness accurately and identifying where your child falls along that spectrum, you can be better equipped with the right responses. Mild shyness may need little intervention. However, severe anxiety requires professional support, with various options in between.

By distinguishing shyness from introversion objectively using assessment tools like the SAS-A, we obtain data to guide appropriate support responses. We also must incorporate research insights into the neurobiology underlying shyness. Science helps us tailor interventions and have realistic expectations.

With accurate working knowledge of your shy child's needs, you can then create plans and situations for them to increase in confidence, develop their social skills expansion, and learn calming strategies. Small victories buoy emotional resilience to counter biologically rooted fear reactions. Our shy children can blossom with patience and compassion. The requisite knowledge begins here.

Equally important, we must challenge prevalent myths that shy children simply need to "get over it," don't want relationships, or could easily change if they tried harder. The reality is much more nuanced. With sensitive understanding, we can help our shy kids feel socially fulfilled by meeting them where they are developmentally. Patience, not pressure, is key, along with evidence-based strategies tailored to their needs.

The knowledge we've gained here lays the foundation to advocate for our shy children compassionately. Armed with better truth and understanding, we can now nurture their emotional growth while building confidence. Ongoing trial and error will happen, but understanding shyness accurately sets us up for social support success.

Chapter 2:

Why Confidence Is Important and How It May Impact a Child's Development and Progress

Between ages 6 and 12, children undergo rapid emotional, social, and intellectual changes instrumental to their lifelong development. Experiences during these formative years greatly influence their adolescent and adult identities and relationships. That's why building confidence to communicate and connect is important. Research shows that skills established in middle childhood shape a child's trajectory for years to come (Gifford-Smith & Brownell, 2003).

Why is this window between ages 6 and 12 so pivotal in shaping life paths? What core skills develop during this timeframe, and why do they matter? How can setbacks now cascade into later mental health struggles?

Understanding the importance of middle childhood milestones is key so we can prioritize nurturing social-emotional intelligence currently. This chapter will explore why speaking up confidently to peers, teachers, and within themselves determines their future academic and relationship success.

Social and Emotional Importance

Forming friendships becomes increasingly essential in middle childhood, as peers replace parents as primary influences. Through play, conversation, and common interests, children discover their identities and values while learning collaboration, conflict resolution, and empathy. Confident communication allows kids to navigate these social intricacies successfully. Close childhood friends build loyalty, teach conflict management, and allow kids to take social-emotional risks within a safe environment. Such experiences cement critical abilities that determine their quality of life down the road.

Through collaborative play, values-driven conversations about fairness, and growing interests, kids learn to relate to different people while finding their place among their peers. Shared problem-solving around relationship conflicts teaches compromise that is fundamental to adult workplace interactions and romantic partnerships. Mentally gearing up to join groups independently rather than depending on parents builds their confidence to initiate purposeful interactions throughout life.

In fact, research links childhood social hesitation to an increased likelihood of adult anxiety disorders, depression, and lower career trajectory and relationship satisfaction (Jones & Gordon, 2016). Painful school memories get reinforced until they feel impossible to overcome without early intervention. Skills stagnating between ages 6 and 12 jeopardize emotional health for years after.

But these social skills require confidence to interact comfortably, articulate thoughts, collaborate on teams, and stand up to peer pressure. Shy kids who avoid social risks may suffer anxiety from missing these pivotal growth opportunities. Developing the confidence to take social-emotional risks now prevents challenges down the road. Without the ability to practice risk-taking among peers, children can struggle with independent decision-making and self-advocacy later on. In fact, research links childhood social hesitation to an increased likelihood of adult anxiety disorders, depression, and lower career success.

The tween and early teen years bring complex social dynamics that demand emotional intelligence and social awareness. Finding one's place among various peer groups, forging close friendships, and learning to lead as well as follow are essential lessons that occur through day-to-day social interactions. Children must speak up with self-assurance to become competent at conflict resolution, standing up to exclusion or bullying, pursuing shared interests, and more. Those lacking the confidence to engage miss out on a lot of cultivating social competence during this critical window. The hallmarks of popularity, leadership charisma, and likeability are established during this time.

Why Speaking Up Matters

Why does assertive communication matter so much between ages 6 and 12, beyond making friends? What's the big deal if kids read quietly at recess instead of chatting? Why push shy children to share their ideas, ask for help at school, or engage peers more actively? There are many reasons for this.

Brain Growth Needs Use

Neural networks governing social and emotional intelligence show rapid growth between ages 6 and 12 but only with consistent practice. It's a pivotal "use it or lose it" window. Young brains struggling to express thoughts, emotions, or needs out loud don't wire these connections sufficiently for fluency later on. Confident self-expression feeds healthy brain development.

Feedback Shapes Identity

Expressing preferences, goals, and beliefs out loud and then integrating others' reactions to them helps children refine their sense of self. By verbalizing their authentic inner voice frequently, kids learn to filter feedback effectively and more maturely. This builds identity integrity and independence. Quiet kids who are denied the opportunity to speak up for themselves and share their opinions struggle internally to define their worth.

New Coping Strategies Emerge

Responding to stressors like being ignored by others, arguments, or academic pressure prompts emotional growth. Managing conflict maturely relies on articulating their feelings and needs constructively. Facing rather than avoiding challenges lets kids add new coping tools that will benefit them for years to come. However, shy kids need support in taking risks and sharing when they feel vulnerable. This, in turn, makes them more resilient.

Overall Wellness Suffers

Studies reveal that children lacking social-emotional outlets like friendships or comfortable class participation experience higher anxiety, depression, and distress throughout development, especially in adolescence. Isolation and lingering hesitation negatively impact self-worth over time without support. Confidence is the preventative medicine.

The reasons confident self-expression, class participation, and social boldness matter before age 12 are many and varied. Communication is important to our children's well-being. Our priorities must reflect that in how we support our children.

Why Confidence Matters

Speaking up confidently between ages 6 and 12 builds skills that influence a child's future path. Here's why it has a big impact: Vocal interaction shapes development in multiple key domains, from relationships to resilience to learning.

Shapes Friendships

Kids learn loyalty, empathy, problem-solving, and standing up for themselves through back-and-forth banter practicing these. Quiet kids miss out on shaping these lifelong skills. Without an opportunity to negotiate conflicts or advocate needs among peers early on, children often struggle with healthy interpersonal dynamics later as teens and adults. These formative social opportunities build trust and conflict resolution abilities that will guide them for decades to come in both platonic and romantic bonds.

Grows the Brain

Brain centers for expression and emotion grow rapidly but need regular use. Putting feelings into words wires vital neural pathways for processing thoughts and feelings long term. Neural connectivity in these regions reaches 80–90% of adult levels by age 12, laying the framework for social-emotional health throughout life. Habitual verbal sharing and processing cultivates confidence and ability in kids and stays with them permanently.

Boosts Coping Abilities

By taking risks among friends to share mistakes, jealousies, or grief, children expand their resilience tool kit to manage stress. These tools carry them through future life storms. Socially supporting one another through painful exclusion, arguments, or embarrassment helps normalize adversity, which is critical for resilience later when stakes seem higher as teens. We build psychological immune strength when given space to safely process when we are upset out loud without judgment.

Supports Learning

Asking teachers questions, collaborating on projects out loud, and speaking to the class sharpens cognitive capacities to excel in later academics and jobs where clear communication is key. Classroom confidence cements intellectual risk-taking, which enables children to have more creative outputs and start to develop some leadership skills that can benefit them later in life as adults. Studies reveal kids able to advocate their academic needs have better memory, verbal scores, curiosity, and course grades through college (Harris, 2018).

The reasons are clear: Nurturing verbal confidence now pays off in friendships, neural growth, managing emotions, and academic achievement affecting kids well into adulthood. Helping shy kids find their voice is an invaluable gift.

Academic Relevance

As school academics become more challenging, success often depends on confident communication abilities. Writing complex arguments, collaborating on group projects, speaking up in class, presenting to peers, and advocating their needs to teachers all require assertiveness. Classroom confidence establishes critical lifelong habits. Educational research confirms this strong correlation between academic risk-taking and achievement.

Additionally, forming bonds with classmates provides emotional support to tackle challenging curriculum. Children who confidently interact access help more easily from peers and teachers. Otherwise, they may fall behind or dread school. If students feel unsafe speaking honestly among classmates, emotional vulnerabilities can easily disrupt learning. Trusted peer groups help students feel understood rather than face school challenges alone.

Raising one's hand to ask clarifying questions also builds the ability to understand complex material independently later in high school and college. Students able to self-monitor comprehension and articulate confusion constructively gain invaluable lifelong learning skills, while quiet, struggling students often fall irrevocably behind.

Presenting projects in front of the class may spark interest and develop talents benefiting future academic and career goals, too. Public speaking and explaining data visually are skills that will transfer broadly across disciplines into adulthood. Yet shy students thinking, *I'm just not good at speaking to groups* may avoid opportunities and lose out on potential opportunities for things that they enjoy.

As students progress throughout school, they will have increasing independence and responsibility. Whether asking a teacher to clarify confusing lesson concepts, collaborating with peers to decipher a writing prompt, or pushing oneself to share work publicly, academic confidence is a prerequisite for achievement. Students who hesitate to answer questions in class miss opportunities to grow intellectually, and those afraid to ask for help when stuck inevitably struggle through lessons alone. Promoting more confident academic communication starting in late childhood is essential. Several studies reveal that confident and assertive students earn better grades than equally intelligent but shy peers.

Impending Adolescence

The tween years—bringing intense physical, emotional, and social changes—approach quickly. Navigating middle school friendships, forging identity, speaking out against bullying, taking academic risks, and coping with confusion all demand substantial confidence. Self-assurance during difficult situations will enable kids to transition more smoothly. Child development experts caution that those not sufficiently self-assured by age 12 will suffer significantly more peer rejection, isolation, and learning gaps in adolescence.

If children don't develop more resilient self-assurance now, the confusion of adolescence can overwhelm them entirely. Building communication confidence and social competence helps kids weather storms ahead. Without adequate coping strategies in place, teen troubles can derail even the most capable students. Studies alarmingly show doubled rates of clinical anxiety and depression among teenagers who lacked social support structures during their middle childhood years.

Pre-teen kids able to joke comfortably with classmates may better handle pressing awkward topics of conversation they might face. Kids comfortable advocating their needs can access health resources proactively before small concerns snowball. And tweens who are practiced in resolving arguments may prevent high school bullying from getting out of hand.

Consider Emily, 12, who loved reading vampire fiction throughout early childhood but hid her niche interest from classmates. When *Twilight* books became popular in middle school, previously judgmental peers now admired her existing knowledge on the topic. But Emily still couldn't engage comfortably about her longtime fascination, losing out on social confidence and assurance she could have gained all along.

Puberty ushers in a whole period of awkwardness, uncertainty, and angst even for relatively confident children. Those who still struggle to speak up socially or assert academic needs at school face much more distressing hurdles ahead. The middle school environment brings advanced coursework, increased peer competitiveness, bullying, exclusion, budding sexuality, comparisons, and confusion. Students require a well-developed sense of identity, priorities, and the ability to emerge on solid ground. Building communication confidence ahead of time is crucial insurance against middle school pitfalls. Researchers emphasize that soft skills like assertiveness and resilience may impact students' high school and college trajectories even more than purely academic talents.

Confidence enables children to access emotional support, academic help, and social belonging critical for thriving currently and into the future. Don't wait, nurture social and emotional confidence now before puberty hits. Building skills ahead of time makes all the difference. Study after study emphasizes that the window between ages 6 and 12 represents an invaluable opportunity to influence a child's entire future well-being.

Case Study: Michael

Michael is a bright 9-year-old who has struggled to make friends since first grade. At the playground, he looks longingly as his classmates chatter and play games together. But he hesitates to join groups, unsure what to say and nervous about rejection. He spends most recesses reading by himself instead, despite wishing to connect with peers.

In class, Michael understands the material but never raises his hand to participate. When the teacher calls on him, he often looks down and mumbles brief responses. For group projects, Michael relies on partners to present his excellent ideas as he stands by silently. He volunteers no opinions during discussions. While clearly engaged and thoughtful, Michael simply lacks the confidence to interact openly. His innate shyness should not be mislabeled as disinterest or incompetence.

His parents have noticed Michael rarely asks friends over or gets invited to social events outside school. They want to nurture more genuine self-assurance before middle school begins, and this becomes even more important as peer relationships and academic pressures intensify. Building social-emotional skills now also prepares Michael to handle exclusion, comparisons, competition, and self-doubt when adolescence strikes. As we've seen, child development research shows that skills developed between ages 6 and 12 form the core of teen and adult relationship success.

Michael's parents realized that by identifying his shyness as mere introversion, they missed the depth of his anxiety and desire to connect meaningfully with peers. They want Michael to develop interests, resilience, empathy, and leadership inherent in childhood friendships. His unease in speaking up threatened later academic progress, too, as the curriculum relies more on confident conversation and team collaboration. His needs for safety and belonging go unmet without secure social bonds.

To fully emerge from his shell in the years ahead, Michael first required targeted support to communicate assertively, take social risks within his stretch zone, and act on ambitions he was starting to think about. Getting these building blocks firmly in place sustainably empowered Michael to manage pending academic and puberty changes. His parents wish they had prioritized social-emotional confidence sooner given its critical long-term influence. Emotional intelligence proves more predictive of adult success than academic marks alone.

Case Study: Sophia

Sophia is a thoughtful 8-year-old who observes classroom dynamics quietly. While clearly taking everything in, she rarely participates verbally. At recess, Sophia reads fiction books while her classmates play sports boisterously. She seems content but lacks close companions during her free time.

In class, Sophia understands concepts but doesn't volunteer answers or ask questions even when confused. For group work, she relies on partners to present her carefully researched ideas. Though engaged intellectually, her hesitancy to speak up limits leadership practice.

Socially, Sophia struggles to initiate conversations or invite new friends over. When her one main friend moved away, Sophia grew more withdrawn. Her parents notice she now fixates on fantasy characters in books since making new real friends feels too intimidating.

Her parents want to prioritize building skills now strengthening identity, resilience, and social circles to prevent adolescent difficulties down the road. They wish they had recognized the pivotal developmental window that ages 6 and 12 represented earlier rather than minimizing and mistaking her shyness as harmless.

Collaborating with Sophia's teacher, her parents enrolled her in a small peer social skills group to practice expressing herself more confidently through role plays. They coach Sophia on taking academic risks like sharing ideas aloud even if she stumbles sometimes. Demonstrating their own vulnerabilities and praise for her effort instead of achieving perfection helps Sophia.

While slow-moving, with compassionate support, Sophia has made gradual but meaningful progress across environments. Nurturing her blossoming assertiveness and friendships during this key childhood window plants seeds securing her growth in the years ahead. Her parents now appreciate that influencing development today impacts life trajectories positively.

Opportunities Abound

The middle childhood years between 6 and 12 represent a pivotal window of opportunity in a child's development. During this time, kids undergo intense changes socially, emotionally, and intellectually that shape their adolescent and adult trajectories.

The developmental biology that comes with childhood confidence demonstrates clearly why this stage matters for emotional health. Neural connectivity, identity formation, and coping strategies developing currently build capacity determining adolescent and adult mental wellness trajectories.

We support early academic abilities knowing they enable later success, so let's now match that diligence in nurturing our child's communication confidence, which matters even more.

Appreciating the irrefutable and accepting the data compels us to act with urgency. Our children's lifelong resilience depends deeply on the priorities we set today. This window between ages 6 and 12 represents a precious opportunity we cannot get back.

That's why nurturing confident communication and emotional competence right now is so critical. Forming secure friendships, taking academic risks, articulating needs clearly, and coping with disappointment all rely on foundational skills cultivated in the present.

Shy or hesitant children who don't get support building social courage and resilience face much greater struggles in the years ahead. The turbulence of middle school, young adulthood, and beyond can overwhelm those lacking self-assurance.

As parents or caregivers, we play an invaluable role in advocating for our kids' developmental needs at this age. By arming ourselves with knowledge of childhood milestones, we can make informed choices to help our children thrive both now and in the future.

Whether enrolling them in social skills groups, pushing gentle encouragement, or working closely with teachers, the effort pays untold dividends when it comes to influencing their development and future. Don't wait; the time is now to plant seeds of confidence and competence crucial for growth.

Our kids navigate increasingly complicated situations during the childhood decade. This chapter aimed to reveal why social-emotional intelligence deserves as much nurturing as academic skills to steer them on the best path ahead.

Support them now and ensure they grow with confidence for years to come.

Chapter 3:

Recognizing the Signs in Your Child

Noticing symptoms of shyness, social anxiety, and lack of confidence in your child is the critical first step to getting them help. Children exhibit behavioral and emotional signals that can indicate difficulties participating socially, interacting comfortably with others, asserting themselves, or managing unfamiliar situations. Recognizing key signs lays the groundwork for addressing underlying causes, building skills, and nurturing confidence.

This chapter covers how to recognize common telltale indicators that your child may be shy, socially on edge, or lacking self-assurance. We'll explore the role personality plays, how to distinguish typical shyness from more severe social anxiety, and what level of struggle requires seeking professional support. Stepping in early when you spot symptoms prevents future challenges and teaches healthy social-emotional coping. Let's explore the core signs to look out for.

How to Recognize That a Child Is Shy and Lacking in Social Confidence

Some common signs can indicate your child is struggling with shyness and hesitancy in social situations. Your child may try to avoid social situations that make them uncomfortable, such as group activities, meeting new people, speaking up in class, or attending parties. They may make excuses to get out of these interactions, such as pretending to feel sick, forgetting about an event, or outright refusing to participate. Noticing a pattern of avoidance behavior is an important red flag that your child feels socially anxious.

You may notice your child is extremely quiet around unfamiliar people and in unfamiliar settings. While some children are naturally less talkative, excessive quietness and hesitancy to speak up may reflect social discomfort. A shy child will be very reluctant to ask questions, answer direct questions, share their opinion, or chat casually in group settings. Simple things like ordering food in public may cause them distress. Observing them staying completely silent while peers around them happily chat is a key sign.

- **Physical signs:** Look for signs your child feels nervous or anxious in social settings. These could include difficulty making eye contact, fidgeting, nail-biting, trembling hands, blushing, sweating, or even stomach aches or headaches. You may also notice quickened breathing, shaky voice, or clenching their fists tightly out of distress. These anxious behaviors tend to increase as social pressure and expectations to participate rise for them.

- **Excessive isolation:** While children need some alone time, excessive isolation from peers for long periods may indicate your child feels safer alone than socializing. A socially hesitant shy child will opt to eat lunch alone, play by themselves at recess, and avoid joining group activities or games. They have very few, if any, friends they interact with regularly. This preference to remain isolated rather than interact can stem from underlying social anxiety.

- **Trouble asserting themselves:** Children lacking social confidence may have difficulty asserting their needs and opinions around others. They may easily give in to peer pressure, afraid to disagree or risk disapproval. You'll observe them going along with the group even if it means hiding their real preferences. They will also struggle to speak up for themselves to authority figures such as coaches or teachers.

- **Poor eye contact:** Socially hesitant children often avoid making eye contact, keeping their gaze downcast around unfamiliar people or groups. Limited eye contact can affect building connections. A shy child will physically turn their head or avert their gaze when speaking to someone, rather than maintaining a natural eye level position. Pressuring them to make eye contact often increases visible signs of nervousness.

- **Excessive school avoidance:** Through sickness claims, skipping classes, or regularly arriving late, this signals the dread that your child might have facing the social and performance elements of school. Missing important instructions or information through missing class then compounds the anxiety.

- **Frequent visits to the nurse's office:** Complaining of stomach aches, headaches, and nausea when no medical explanation suffices may indicate social stress affects their physical health. Ask the nurse to track visit times and symptoms.

If you've noticed a pattern of social struggle and several of these signs in your child, it may indicate underlying shyness and low social confidence requiring support. Catching and addressing it early on can prevent future social challenges that could negatively impact their development. Recognizing the symptoms is the critical first step toward helping your shy child become more confident.

Where Does Personality Fit Into Shyness?

A child's natural personality can play a major role in contributing to shyness and social hesitancy. Personality refers to someone's basic disposition and patterns of how they react to emotions. Children have different personalities—some are outgoing while others are reserved by nature. Shy children tend to have slow-to-warm-up personalities, where they need extended time to establish comfort with new people or new social situations before exhibiting their true outgoing personality. Pushing them to warm up faster than their natural pace often backfires, leading to increased distress.

Children with **slow-to-warm-up personalities** tend to be more socially cautious and shy. They feel uncomfortable in new social situations and scenarios that make them the center of attention. These children need time to observe a setting before joining in, prefer familiar environments, and slowly open up over multiple interactions. Forcing them into unfamiliar, spotlighted scenarios very quickly will likely overwhelm them. Meeting new friends may take weeks or months rather than minutes or hours.

Similarly, children with **high-sensitivity personalities** may also be prone to shyness. Highly sensitive children are very perceptive of social cues and emotionally reactive. They tend to easily feel overwhelmed by noisy busy settings and too much social stimulation. Loud chaotic environments like playgrounds, parties, or group activities exhaust their ability to socialize very quickly. Managing all the dynamics of group social interactions tires their emotional resources quickly, making them withdraw.

While personality doesn't necessarily cause shyness, it can predispose children to be shy, anxious, and uncertain in some social situations. Their biological makeup prompts them to respond and behave shyly when feeling uncomfortable, unsure, or overstimulated. Recognizing your child's personality provides insight into why they struggle in certain scenarios and how to best support them. Addressing situations that trigger their sensitivity and shyness is key while also nurturing confidence. With patience and compassion for their personality, shy children can learn to manage social challenges.

Distinction Between Shyness and Lack of Social Confidence With Social Anxiety

While shyness, lack of confidence, and social anxiety have overlapping qualities, there are some distinctions between them to note.

Shyness

Shyness refers to feelings of hesitation, uncertainty, and mild discomfort in new or unfamiliar social settings where the focus is on oneself. However, shyness tends to go away once a child feels more comfortable and confident. With support, shy children can learn to adapt. A shy child will exhibit some nervous behaviors when first meeting someone or entering an unfamiliar setting, but be able to relax and open up after adjusting to the new situation.

Lack of Social Confidence

Lack of social confidence involves difficulties asserting oneself socially and navigating interpersonal dynamics. However, confidence can grow considerably through practice and positive experiences that teach missing skills. A child lacking confidence just needs more opportunities to safely practice social skills and gain competence. As they repeat positive social exchanges, confidence steadily builds.

Social Anxiety Disorder

Social anxiety disorder, however, reflects consistent, intense anxiety when facing social interactions and being around others paired with a strong fear of embarrassment or judgment. It persists despite repeated exposures and disrupts daily functioning at home, school, or recreational settings. A socially anxious child experiences distress across social situations, even familiar ones, without their anxiety getting much better over time and practice.

Children can be shy while also feeling socially anxious in situations that trigger fears of failure or rejection beyond their capacity to cope. The lines between mild shyness or anxiety and a disorder are often blurred. However, paying attention and addressing patterns of extreme fear early can help you help your child strengthen their resiliency. Monitoring the intensity and persistence of anxiety symptoms can help determine if a disorder is developing that requires professional support.

If your child is avoiding certain situations that become a pattern that is harming and impacting their daily life, it suggests therapy may be needed to address sensitive or anxious tendencies. Tracking severity and durations can determine appropriate levels and types of help. Ordering a simple meal, asking a store clerk a question, or attending a birthday party provoke extreme anxiety disproportionate to the actual situation, prompting avoidance that interferes with daily childhood activities.

The Time to Ask for Professional Help

If your child's shyness and social difficulties persist despite your efforts and begin interfering with their life, it may be time to ask for professional support. Some signs it's time to seek help include:

- Your child avoids or refuses to participate in normal social activities with family, friends, school, or community over an extended time.

- Social isolation and withdrawal grow more severe to where they hardly interact with peers for weeks or months, missing key social connections.

Anxiety about social situations such as attending school, organized activities, or playgrounds provokes intense emotional and physical symptoms prompting avoidance. A racing heart, panicking stomach aches, clingy behavior, tantrums, or meltdowns reflect distress that they can't manage, so they opt out entirely through refusal or avoidance.

Performance in academics declines because social aspects such as presenting in class, group work with peers, or asking questions severely cause distress. Poor grades result from skipping classes, strained peer collaboration, and debilitating test anxiety requiring extra support to be successful in the classroom.

Signs of depression emerge, lack of interest in previously enjoyed activities, low mood and irritability, sleep or appetite changes, and expressing hopeless feelings about their social struggles. Loss of pleasure, isolation, acting out anger over social stress, and dark statements about themselves or the future require an immediate response.

Seeking counseling can help objectively assess your child's social abilities and challenges, determine any underlying disorders, and establish customized treatment plans catered to their needs, which may include social skills training, counseling, or other tiered interventions matching severity. Early specialized support teaches tools to manage social anxiety and build confidence to prevent future struggles. An outside professional perspective provides greater insight into the root causes impairing healthy development so appropriate help can begin in the more extreme cases.

Case Study: Alex

Alex is a quiet 8-year-old who has always preferred solitary activities like reading over social situations. His parents put it down to a shy, introverted temperament. But in second grade, he began exhibiting intense distress around attending school.

Each morning, Alex would share complaints of exhaustion, stomach aches, or headaches to stay home. At school events, he hid behind his parents declining to participate. He used to love learning but his grades dropped off as he skipped more classes.

Attempts to arrange play dates were met with strong reluctance. Alex often opted to play alone, rarely interacting with peers even when they approached him. He sat alone at recess reading books and in silence.

His parents grew very concerned when Alex declared he had no friends and felt hopeless about that changing. He burst into tears when they gently encouraged him to practice talking with others. Alex insisted something was "wrong" with him for being so scared to talk.

All of these signs indicated Alex's temperamental shyness had evolved into extreme social anxiety and poor self-esteem interfering with him being able to be a happy little boy. After seeking counseling, Alex was assessed as likely having social anxiety disorder.

With treatment incorporating exposure therapy, social skills development, and building self-compassion, Alex slowly strengthened his social confidence within a year. Support groups connected him with friends and peers conquering similar struggles, building motivation.

Today, Alex can interact comfortably with friends, participate in class discussions, and attend social functions without debilitating distress. When reflecting on his childhood, he credits his parents' early intervention for getting him life-changing help and has become an advocate for recognizing symptoms of childhood anxiety.

Case Study: Emma

Emma is a 7-year-old girl who has always been exceptionally shy and quiet. At school, she avoids speaking up in class and isolates herself at recess, reading books alone. Her teacher noticed Emma lacks the confidence to interact with peers, answer or ask questions, or join group play.

At home, Emma's parents observed similar social hesitancy. Playdates provoked tears and meltdowns. Emma once vomited from nerves before a birthday party and refused to attend another one for a year. In public, Emma clings anxiously to her parents, hiding behind their legs.

While Chloe and Ryan knew Emma was shy, second grade revealed new extreme avoidance. Emma faked frequent sick days to skip school. She stopped trying to make friends altogether, insisting something was "wrong with her." Her isolation and distress concerned Chloe and Ryan more than the shyness itself.

Tracking symptoms revealed Emma's shyness now prevented normal childhood activities at home and school. After comparing behavioral checklists, they sought counseling support. An assessment confirmed Emma likely had social anxiety disorder requiring treatment.

With therapy plus practicing social skills in small groups, Emma slowly strengthened confidence, speaking up and relating to peers. Learning tools that enabled her to manage her nerves allowed her to participate in class again. Support groups reduced her feeling of being alone. Today Emma still prefers quiet but can attend social events and interact with friends without intense suffering.

Emma's parents credit early vigilance in spotting social distress for preventing worse future struggles. Noticing signs of shyness evolving into anxiety allowed early intervention that set Emma up to thrive again. Their compassion in reading clues that she used to mask her anxiety paved the way toward confidence.

Observational Awareness

Noticing symptoms of social anxiety or extreme shyness is crucial yet challenging. Even children craving connection may hide how they're feeling inside. Setting aside consistent observation time, tracking patterns over weeks, and reviewing symptom checklists equips you to uncover hidden signs that something is amiss. Early detection paves the way for life-changing interventions before small struggles become lifelong challenges. Your compassion and commitment to reading those subtle clues can help a withdrawn child blossom into their vibrant social self.

Chapter 4:

Creating a Supportive and Encouraging Environment

Creating an encouraging environment is the foundation where shy children's confidence and skills can bloom. Their growth depends not just on targeted parenting interventions but on the entire ecosystem surrounding and shaping them daily. This chapter explores practical, holistic strategies to ensure your home encourages and supports the assurance a hesitant child requires.

We'll cover how to model assertiveness to your child while also respecting their temperament, encourage interests that make connecting more comfortable, praise effort over traits, and shift mindsets toward growth possibility. Environment is the critical force quietly cultivating or hindering self-belief. Let's shape an empowering one embracing where our shy kids are now and how they can progress.

Teaching Assertiveness and Self-Confidence

Assertiveness involves confidently communicating your thoughts and feelings in a clear, respectful way. A supportive, encouraging environment provides a strong foundation for assertiveness and self-confidence to take root in a shy child. Children learn assertiveness and self-confidence through observing others who are assertive and self-confident, nurturing practice, and celebrating small wins. Use descriptive praise to highlight small moments of assertiveness, no matter how subtle, to positively reinforce baby steps. Praise children for having the courage to speak up instead of criticizing how they say it. This will help them feel more comfortable being assertive.

Show examples of clear, respectful assertiveness around your child frequently. Calmly advocate for your needs, ask clarifying questions, and resolve conflicts maturely with others. Show confidence by speaking up politely. Your example demonstrates crucial skills shaping their behavior. Allow them to witness you navigating tricky social situations with grace and finesse, showcasing diplomacy in action. Break down your self-assured approach into clear and actionable steps:

- Coach them privately to repeat requests if ignored until their request is heard and addressed. Practicing clarity and persistence without aggression in safe settings makes your child feel that they can try to be assertive and build their confidence.

- Role-play scenarios that feel challenging so they can rehearse responses that feel authentic to their personality and the types of situations that they might face, like in school. Help them start to feel the value and confidence in being assertive.

- Highlight achievements and positive qualities often, keeping criticism minimal. Counter their negative self-talk by emphasizing their strengths. Boosting self-worth and drowning out their inner voices urging them to be silent is key. Redirect their focus to examples of social success when nerves strike so that their confidence can outweigh doubt.

Giving very shy children lots of small opportunities to practice standing up for themselves while offering steady encouragement can help them develop skills for expressing themselves properly. As confidence in their thoughts, feelings, and abilities grows, so will their ability to voice them. Give them time to develop their self-confidence by remaining patient; growth won't happen overnight, but each small gain builds toward social confidence.

Encouraging Activities, Interests, and Hobbies

Cultivating activities, passions, and hobbies that your child enjoys can greatly help strengthen their confidence and social skills. Focus on their natural talents and what sparks positivity. Tap into what brings them joy and makes their eyes light up rather than what seems impressive. Be led by their delight rather than society's standards. What matters most is that an interest feels inspiring through their unique eyes on the world.

Help discover activities matching their temperament where they won't feel spotlight pressure. Gentle interests like art, music, animals, and nature often appeal. Ensure programs nurture self-esteem. Shy children thrive in supportive communities focused on growth rather than how they are strictly being measured on their performance. Assist them in finding warm, welcoming environments to explore interests at their own pace.

Find peers sharing similar interests via classes or community groups. Bonding over common passions feels more comfortable than forced friendships. They can practice socializing without difficult small talk. Shared activities provide natural conversation starters, so connections can be built naturally. Support fostering friendships through suitable social channels lining up with their personality.

Let them learn at their own pace without criticism. Support exploring new hobbies without judgment if they decide to give them up. The goal is to enjoy the process, not perfection. Remember to praise effort and dedication over talent and outcomes. Demonstrate how to accept mistakes and setbacks as part of the learning adventure. Change course to overcome roadblocks rather than assigning blame or shame that they don't feel that they can manage or overcome.

As children grow through interests they feel continually successful at, they take in important messages that build confidence, such as "I have valuable skills," "I can connect with others meaningfully," and "I accomplish great things through dedication." Nurturing personal passions on their terms teaches shy children important life lessons beyond social confidence. Interests that align with their personality help reinforce their identity as capable, interesting people with much to offer the world.

Nurturing Growth

Nurturing a shy child's growth requires delicacy, empathy, and respect for their pace. Pressuring them to adopt an extroverted persona often backfires, increasing self-consciousness and anxiety. Their relief stems from accepting rather than trying to change their temperament. Celebrate small displays of courage while minimizing unnecessary spotlights. Help them feel seen and valued for who they are behind their shyness rather than just what others can see.

Help them to realize that being introverted is just as good as being extroverted; it's just different. Introverts aren't lacking anything; they simply need less social contact and more quiet time to feel energized. Try to adjust to faster-paced family routines so introverts' needs are respected, too. Share examples of famous introverts who used alone time to fuel success. Picturing futures suited to who they are deep down takes away the pressure introverts often feel to act extroverted.

Listen without judgment and validate the emotions that challenge them. Instead of downplaying or dismissing the anxiety they feel, respond with understanding and gently help them think about it more positively. Help them verbally express and process fears or anxieties before, during, and after difficult social situations. Reviewing and discussing their experiences together builds trust and clarity.

Allow quiet participation in group activities without criticism. Gradually encourage small steps forward when they are ready, like briefly joining conversations, not dominating them. Praise efforts to interact while ensuring a safe emotional space if they feel overwhelmed. Empower their choices by permitting them to withdraw or have a break, without criticizing them—but encourage them to keep trying!

With supportive patience and space to slowly warm up socially over time instead of expecting an instant change, shy children gain the courage to integrate self-acceptance into their daily interactions with others. Focus nurturing care on helping them see their sensitivity as a strength. As they develop more self-compassion, they will also become more compassionate toward others. This completes the cycle of giving and receiving care.

Helping Develop and Encourage a Growth Mindset

Shifting shy children's mindsets from self-limiting to being growth-focused is essential for confidence. Fixed mindsets assume personality traits like shyness can't change, sabotaging motivation and the courage and willingness to develop their confidence. Growth mindsets believe personal qualities can evolve with effort over time. Encourage them to understand this encouraging perspective. Teach children that their brains are capable of changing with intentional practice. Help them view themselves as works in progress rather than finished products.

Reinforce that the brain keeps growing rapidly in childhood. New experiences literally reshape it. Describe shyness as a sign that their sensitive, observant brain is still learning how to adapt to social situations, not a permanent flaw. Use metaphors like growing their brain muscles through new challenges and practice. Help them see shyness as just how their brain is wired, not something wrong with who they are.

Separate actions from identity constantly with a strengths focus. They did something shy; they aren't inherently shy. Emphasize choice, effort, and flexible responses charting improvement, not static labels. Write out talking points together they can repeat if you are concerned that criticism will become something that they won't be able to put into perspective, "I'm practicing a skill in progress; this doesn't define me."

Demonstrate any setbacks or difficult situations they didn't manage well during social situations as feedback for learning, not proof of permanent failure due to bad personality. Teach kids to change their approach based on results rather than being too hard on themselves if early efforts don't go perfectly. Openly discuss your own growth processes to normalize struggle as part of progress.

Celebrate small, incremental wins while keeping perspective on progress made in growth journeys that ebb and flow. What seems insignificant to others can feel like a major triumph that quiet children privately celebrate as they are focusing on increasing their confidence. Help them track milestones by looking backward and forward so nothing feels impossible.

The pathway is long, but focusing ahead can make their destiny feel more hopeful and less constrained if they look toward expanding their potential rather than accepting what they feel are limitations that will hold them back. Progress quickens when mindsets embrace change. Plant seeds of aspiration by talking to them about role models who transformed shyness into strength, such as icons of influence like Daniel Radcliffe and Rhianna.

The Crucial Role of Schools

While parents lay the foundation of secure attachment and unconditional belief instilling confidence at home, children spend the bulk of their time at school. Teachers and school communities must also foster inclusive, identity-safe spaces embracing diverse dispositions without judgment. Let's explore the pivotal role educational ecosystems play in positively influencing shy students' potential.

Setting the Tone

Teachers set the emotional tone within classrooms through their policies, practices, and responses to demonstrate acceptance daily. Warmly greeting all students at the door, learning preferred names and pronouns, and allowing movement breaks and quiet spaces demonstrate that well-being trumps rigid control. Privately checking in with hesitant students weekly before anxiety sets in fosters trusting partnerships. Simply asking "How can I support you feeling safe and successful here?" can shift the dynamics profoundly.

Curriculum Considerations

Offering clear expectations, rubrics, and rationale will reduce the uncertainty that a shy or anxious child might have, which can paralyze them if they are a perfectionist. Sharing lesson content, vocabulary, and discussion prompts ahead prevents their distress. Setting the pace appropriately to master foundational concepts before accelerating will build their confidence. Mixed objective and creative assessments allow personalization. Compassionate curriculum adjustments can facilitate engagement with kids and their willingness to speak up more confidently.

Peers Can Help

Teachers hold power facilitating inclusion and destigmatizing shyness among peers. Having vocal students share their own hesitancy openly says, "You are not alone." Classrooms with many personalities demonstrate diversity. Role-playing responding sensitively to shy classmates makes that caring instinct habitual. Teachers must intentionally nurture empathy alongside academic skills daily. Kids take cues on acceptance from them.

Leverage Staff

Enlist school counselors, social workers, psychologists, and nurses to all collaborate to track struggling students' patterns more holistically. Compare observational trends confidentially across different situations to identify peak stressors. Recess monitors can speak volumes about peer dynamics. Join forces with teachers to advocate for needs children can't. Many shy kids need that collected insight to help everyone decide what actions will help them develop their confidence and thrive.

Partner Proactively

While respecting privacy laws, parents should proactively ask teachers to consistently report back on how their child participates across the day, noting any struggles and strengths. Teachers should educate parents on what quietness signals versus benign preference and share accessible resources like social-emotional learning conversation starters, quiet leadership outlines, or relational aggression guides to guide home support, preventing crises. Parental partnership is pivotal, so parents should take the lead in asking for this information from teachers to best support their child's development. This includes asking teachers to proactively inform them on how their child participates across the day, what quietness may signal about their child, and requesting resources that can aid conversations and support at home.

With open communication and partnership between parents and teachers, we can work together to foster growth.

Adjust Expectations, Not the Child

Rather than pressuring introverts to perform loud extroversion, parents and caregivers should have conversations with schools to understand how participation and assessment standards are determined. They can then discuss adjustments so standards equally value quiet excellence, letting engagement and skill determine metrics rather than style prejudices. Parents should ask how leadership is defined and whether public speaking skills are relevant for future jobs. Broadening definitions of success empowers diverse identities.

School ecosystems can stealthily cultivate confidence when intentionally supportive, not skewed toward narrow definitions of projected outgoing charm. Parents should nurture every child's budding resilience by advocating for space for their authentic emerging selves to stand proudly. The world needs precisely what their sensitive minds hold. Parents can initiate conversations with schools to transform education culture and let their child's inner light shine.

Case Study: Liam

Liam was a shy 7-year-old who avoided speaking up in groups and making new friends. At school, he walked the playground alone, feeling intimidated to join games. His hesitancy in communicating verbally made class participation feel terrifying. Academically capable, Liam struggled in voicing his needs or asking questions.

His parents wanted to pressure Liam into "getting over" his shyness quickly, but his therapist urged understanding his sensitive temperament. She worked with them on tweaking Liam's environment to nurture confidence gently.

They chose gentler-paced activities suiting Liam's introversion like art and chess over noisy team sports. Making friends felt less forced as he found peers who shared similar passions. Small talk wasn't needed when collaborating on projects, easing social connections.

His parents demonstrated politely yet firmly advocating needs in front of Liam. They warmly praised the tiny social steps he attempted without critique. Privately, they role-played speaking up until he felt more comfortable.

Seeing his parents' patience and support, Liam's growth mindset solidified. With practice, he could progress. Counseling helped him to manage any recurring anxiety, which would make him want to give up. Bit by bit, confidence emerged.

While still reserved, Liam can now initiate playground games and speak up for himself appropriately. He takes quiet pride in overcoming fears that previously held him back and continues nurturing his journey at his own pace.

Case Study: Ella

Ella is a quiet 9-year-old who avoids social situations and speaking up at school. While gentle and bright, participating in class and making friends causes Ella severe anxiety resulting in frequent absences. Her parents want to help but aren't sure where to start.

Seeing Ella spend every recess reading alone under a tree, her parents compassionately discuss her struggles with how she verbally expresses herself in groups. They emphasize wanting to understand how to make environments less overwhelming so learning and connecting feel safer. Ella opens up about specific social fears of judgment if she stutters in class and rejection if she asks to join playground games. She despairs that her shyness feels impossible to overcome, isolating her forever.

Her parents respond with empathy, sharing their own insecurities at her age while reassuring her that, with patient practice, social skills can improve over time. They remind Ella that challenges often stem from shyness being a difference, not a deficit. Unique sensitivities become superpowers allowing her to develop deep empathy for others as she grows.

Ella's parents tailor support to her developmental stage, rehearsing small talk scripts about favorite books to more comfortably befriend kindred peers. Finding a read-aloud group focused on growth over perfection helps too. To curb classroom anxiety, they collaborate with the teacher and request lessons be shared ahead of time allowing low-stress previewing. Monthly meetings with her compassionate teacher, Ms. Bell, build trust.

Ella made a few close friends by reaching out to a girl with Hello Kitty sneakers about their shared adoration. Now when overstimulated socially, she practices calming strategies like mindful breathing rather than self-attack. Ella grows more patient with and proud of her sensitive self, blossoming healthily in her own introverted way on her timeline.

Environment Matters

The places where shy kids spend time each day matter more than any advice we give. Home, school, and activities—these environments shape their deep beliefs in what they can do.

Children absorb messages from what people around them say, how they act, and what they praise and criticize. They take in attitudes about different personality types based on how others relate to them. They adopt beliefs about their potential from what opportunities and options they see available to them. Kids soak it all up quietly.

Take a careful look at what your shy child hears, sees, and experiences day to day:

- Do they see role models overcoming challenges with effort?

- Do images and stories show that quiet skills are valued, too?

- Do peers and teachers accept differences without teasing?

- Is hard work praised more than perfect grades?

- Is speaking up encouraged gently rather than forced?

Tweaking environments teaches as much as our words.

Think also about the even bigger culture that kids are immersed in from media and public figures. Does it embrace introverts positively? Do influential leaders demonstrate an understanding of those with other styles? Are supposedly "feminine" traits like compassion and nurturing represented as strengths? We need to examine the unspoken signals and rearrange them to encourage the full spectrum of different personality traits and types.

If we want shy kids to believe in their potential, the worlds surrounding them need to believe in it, too—at home, school, and beyond. The steady power of environment cultivates either courage or doubt deep down. Let's make what they inhale every day shout of possibility!

Chapter 5:

Strategies for Helping Your Child Navigate Social Situations

Supporting your shy children's journey to successfully navigate diverse social situations requires insightfully customizing their environment. From educational settings to playdate approaches, intentionally structuring their interactions mapped to their needs creates the security that unlocks their growth. The goal is to override their paralysis of lack of confidence by slowly and surely increasing their exposure until assurance in their abilities takes hold. Let's cultivate ecosystems where children feeling unsure can safely gain competence by interacting, conversing, and playing. Start by assessing their current struggles to pinpoint priority areas to support their progress. Every child's shy triggers differ, so tune into their unique needs and create the right strategies to help them grow in confidence.

Choosing the Right School and Educational Environment

Selecting an optimal school environment supportive of your shy child's learning and confidence is crucial given the considerable time spent there. Prioritize schools promoting emotional safety through compassionate community and anti-bullying policies. Investigate if these policies translate into genuine culture change by reviewing school climate reports and statistics, as well as having discussions with administrators, teachers, parents, and students rather than surface-level box-checking.

For example, are there student-led anti-bullying initiatives? Do teachers incorporate social-emotional learning into their classrooms? How exactly has the school culture improved? Look for engaged educators motivated to continuously better support all students through collaborating with parents, pursuing professional development opportunities focused on inclusion and empathy, and finding new ways to identify and help struggling students thrive. The practical application of compassionate policies and an engaged, motivated staff can make a world of difference in determining the right school for your shy child.

- Investigate student-teacher ratios allowing personalized attention and partnerships supporting unique needs. Smaller classes and campus sizes help hesitant students feel less overwhelmed. Find out if staff receive regular empathetic communication and trauma-informed care training on nurturing students experiencing social-emotional struggles impacting their learning. Understanding and accommodating needs compassionately should reach every level, from teachers to administrators.

- Inquire about multi-tiered approaches to ease transitions, foster inclusion, and develop student self-advocacy skills. Seek robust counseling teams incorporating individual and group talk therapy sessions, as well as regular check-ins. Look for both proactive and reactive emotional support embedding these concepts into everyday school life through mindfulness practices, classroom discussions, and teaching coping strategies. Initiatives should emphasize emotional wellness shaping the whole child.

- Ask if electives, clubs, and special events encourage bonding over shared interests rather than intimidating social mixing. Can shy students find their niche through activities aligned with their temperament? Make sure this niche building extends beyond the classroom into activities like art club, coding club, theater troupe, and student councils, cementing genuine friendships schoolwide.

- Schedule observations of prospective schools witnessing culture in action. Notice how students interact and support each other through examples by teachers and initiatives led by student leaders. Look for buddy systems pairing older mentors with younger students, cross-age group collaborations on projects, and students spearheading inclusion campaigns. Is diversity, empathy, and sensitivity embedded across school life into the entire school community? The goal is to include all different systems and practices into one harmonious culture to support your child.

The right educational fit helps shy students thrive academically while also steadily developing social-emotional coping skills with guidance tailored to their needs. Prioritize supportive cultures enabling success on your child's terms by ensuring your child feels heard and understood first before strategizing layered success plans tapping into a compassionate, student-centered ecosystem. Then, look at how the school and the student ecosystem play a part in your strategy to support your child.

Encouraging Involvement in Activities, Hobbies, and New Experiences

Cultivating interests and hobbies boosts shy children's confidence while also creating natural paths for social connections. Help discover their passions and possibilities without pressure through open-ended questions about what brings them joy and makes them lose track of time. Provide opportunities like museum visits, community center classes, or at-home craft projects to explore potentials aligned with their temperament and sensory needs.

For example, a child showing attention to detail may enjoy jewelry making or coding. Make gentle suggestions, then let them decide what sparks their enthusiasm without judgment. Sign them up for reasonable commitments without overscheduling by starting with one familiar activity. Provide enthusiastic yet low-key support by attending events without being overbearing and celebrating milestones privately to avoid inadvertent spotlight pressure. Discovering genuine passions nurtures self-esteem, skill-building, and organic social connections.

Find peers sharing similar interests via classes or community groups, such as coding camps, arts and crafts workshops, or book clubs to ease overcoming some of their anxiety and building their confidence through common ground. Bonding over mutual passions feels more comfortable than forced small talk friendships. Guide them toward suitable social channels where they can establish friendships organically over time rather than demanding quick intimacy exceeding their comfort level.

For example, conversation flows more smoothly when focused on a shared activity like learning a new computer program or painting technique. Joining a youth community theater program allows friendships to build slowly while working together toward a common goal. Shared activities make conversations happen organically through a focus on common interests rather than demanding that your shy child feel vulnerable and share a lot about themselves straight away. Book lover groups, coding camps, and other niche interest social channels let them warm up socially at their own pace.

Encourage trying new experiences in bite-sized steps slightly outside their comfort zone that are less likely to be overwhelming. For example, if they are nervous about starting a new sport, go together the first few times until they get more comfortable. Offer to participate side-by-side with your child until they feel ready to independently engage in the activity. If their ultimate goal is attending sleepaway summer camp, break that larger goal down into smaller incremental steps over many months to grow their readiness and excitement versus avoidance.

First, let them attend a local day camp with a friend to get used to being away from home for just a portion of the day. Next, build up to overnight camps that are only one or two nights before eventually reaching a full week or two once they have acquired the coping strategies to manage longer stays. Reflect with them frequently to see how they are feeling after trying new experiences, provide positive feedback, and remind them that they have your support through their journey of experiencing new settings. Celebrate the completion of each small step to further motivate and encourage their growth. Preparing them gradually and reassuring them consistently can transform doubt into confidence through their achievement of goals they once thought impossible.

Focus on enjoying the process rather than achieving perfection when they are attempting new hobbies or challenges. Demonstrate bouncing back from mistakes and discomfort by positively reframing and discussing them with your child as learning opportunities. When setbacks occur, help reframe them not as confirmation of failure but, rather, as constructive feedback they can use for future situations, thus preserving self-motivation and positive self-image.

As they gather small wins and try new things with support, shy children realize they can adapt to unfamiliar situations. Nurturing courage to step forward empowers their journeys toward assuring themselves "I can do this." In time, confident self-talk overrides the inner voice whispers urging they stay hidden: "What if I can't do this? It's safer if I quit." With compassionate encouragement, new confidence and the realization that they can do this emerge.

Organized Playdates and Activities

Thoughtfully planned playdates help shy children practice social skills in a safe, structured environment. This reduces uncertainty and reluctance to participate in social situations. For example, you can maximize a shy child's comfort when arranging get-togethers with unfamiliar peers by getting to know the other child's parents first. Determine if the children's personalities, interests, and energy levels seem reasonably compatible before planning a first playdate. Avoid initially pairing a very outgoing child with an extremely sensitive one, as this is likely to be overwhelming. Openly discuss appropriate expectations with the other parents, ensuring both children's needs will be mutually respected.

Start with one-on-one playdates rather than groups to lower social performance demands and allow your child to focus attention on befriending just one new peer. Host the first few meetings at your home, as the familiar environment helps ease tension and stress. Prepare your child in advance by explaining what to expect so the social situation feels less intimidating and unknown. Offer them coping strategies like taking a quiet break if they feel overwhelmed.

Structure the activities around things your child enjoys during early playdates—like crafts, board games or nature walks—rather than demanding unfamiliar pretend play scenarios requiring more creativity. Join in side-by-side, modeling relaxation through your own calm participation. Avoid overstimulating your child by introducing electronics or other sources of sensory overload. Encourage collaboration on projects like art or building toys that yield natural teamwork opportunities.

Gradually build up to outings once your child's connection with the new friend solidifies. Select destinations well-aligned with their interests that are low in crowds and loud noise. Accompany the children until you can observe your child handling the situation capably on their own. Assess their stamina and enjoyment after social outings to determine the right frequency of get-togethers—balancing growth with adhering to their limits. Celebrate all progress in expanding their comfort zone.

With your careful planning focused on ensuring play feels more enjoyable than exhausting for your shy child, they can expand social skills and circles at their own pace. Provide ongoing support to set them up for successful interactions with peers that end on a positive note, so their confidence builds steadily. The goal is to gently nudge them to stretch their comfort zone through managed exposure experiences.

The Pivotal Role of Parents

While teachers and schools provide critical external ecosystems nurturing shy children's growth, parents create the very first environment shaping the development of confidence and social skills. As primary caregivers, we have a daily influence on the atmosphere around shy kids. Let's explore impactful activities we can embrace to encourage healthy resilience in our kids.

Demonstrate Speaking Up

Children observing parents consistently yet respectfully speak up asking for their needs to be met, resolving conflicts diplomatically, and contributing ideas assertively absorb these communication skills through osmosis. Show how to handle difficult conversations and overcome challenges through courageous vulnerability. Demonstrate polite persistence paired with compassion. Kids witnessing self-assured advocacy from trusted caregivers start to believe in their own voice.

Talk Through Social Struggles

Verbalizing your own childhood shyness or current situations where you are nervous or feel unsure informs children these difficulties are common, temporary, and manageable rather than shameful flaws. Normalize hitting developmental speed bumps by sharing stories to overcome them. Discuss useful strategies to boost confidence that worked for you so children hear specific game plans to build courage through practice and know that they are not alone.

Applaud Small Daily Wins

Quietly praise every tiny social step forward that your child attempts, from briefly joining a playground game to ordering their own snack. Track wins privately through a stealth sticker chart or journal away from criticism. Document those small wins privately with your child, either using stickers or other ways to celebrate this. Consistent celebration of small milestones you notice in your child builds motivation, conquering lingering reluctance through step-by-step progress.

Structure Optimal Conditions

When planning social activities for your shy child, thoughtfully consider their current comfort zone and social-emotional capacity. Aim to stretch their skills gently without becoming overwhelming. For example, carefully plan playdates with one other child first, then slowly expand to small groups as your child is ready. When planning family gatherings, prepare your child for new people or environments that could cause anxiety, and modify or shorten the event if needed to prevent paralyzing distress. Choose extracurriculars intentionally by starting with independent activities or very small groups, then gradually introduce more social interaction as your child's confidence and competence develop further. The goal is to progressively challenge their social stamina so they can build skills over time. Continue shaping social interactions in a caring way that reduces chances of anxiety while expanding your child's ability to handle new situations. Meet them where they are now, nurturing internal growth so their light can shine brighter.

Redirect Critical Messages

Challenge and debate family members, friends, or media voices that judge quiet traits as weaknesses with clear advocacy that sensitivity holds equal value to being loud. Children believing their parents perceive their dispositions as full of potential build resilient self-belief from a strong home base less influenced by outside skepticism.

Collaborate on Coping Skills

Equip children to manage uncertainty through new mental strategies like positive self-talk scripts, visualization of calming spaces, or playful distraction via I Spy. Practice role plays to help your child handle mysteries like new peer groups or school transitions even if they are initially clumsy until imagining uncertainty feels safer. Build up their coping skills so they have a tool kit of strategies as they grow up.

Explore Social Stories

Read books, view films, and engage in personal narratives normalizing shyness through characters overcoming challenges mirroring your child's journey. Seeing heroes tentatively blossom socially will resonate with your child while discovering positive role models persevering beyond fear. Discussions and questions will prompt your child to apply lessons through seeing real-life examples.

Consider Counseling

If lack of confidence and social anxiety persist, heavily impacting home life despite ongoing compassionate efforts, seek professional support assessing the skill gaps needing additional support, like conversational turn-taking or reading facial expressions and body language. Counseling builds missed abilities through expert coaching and tailored reinforcement that your child can then adapt to real-world settings.

Leverage your position as the closest caregiver, understanding the nuances of your shy child's personality. Through steady sharing of examples, structured exposure, skill-building partnerships, and unconditional support, you sculpt home environments that empower the transition from hesitant to confident at their own pace. Environment forms their foundation for building confidence.

Case Study: Noah

Noah was an intellectually gifted 9-year-old who struggled considerably with anxiety and low confidence interacting at school. He yearned to answer questions and contribute to class discussions. But overwhelming self-consciousness led him to stay silent, fading into the background.

Group projects frustrated Noah. The expectation to collaborate seamlessly with classmates he barely knew socially taxed his mental bandwidth. No matter how hard he practiced, conversing with classmates, friends, and the teacher still felt awkward.

At recess, he amused himself alone, too intimidated to approach unfamiliar peers. Having limited common interests with macho sports-loving boys didn't help. Desperately wishing for a friend, Noah instead obsessively read books, seeking fictional bonds with the characters in the books.

His parents recognized Noah's school environment needed to better support his shy, introverted temperament for him to thrive there. After assessing options, they transferred him to a smaller gifted academy with mentoring programs, student-driven electives, and teachers trained in social-emotional learning.

The nurturing environment made all the difference. Noah quickly found his group of friends through bonding over academics and sci-fi. With compassionate coaching, contributing to discussions felt less terrifying. Club activities allowed him to build collaborative skills gradually.

By year's end, Noah had blossomed. Seeing his inner self mirrored and valued in the school community transformed Noah's self-perception from an isolated outcast to feeling like he securely belonged in the school. The right conditions enabled Noah to finally flourish both socially and academically.

Case Study: Lily

Lily is a shy second grader who rarely speaks up at school and struggles to make friends on the chaotic playground. Group projects overwhelmed her. No matter how hard her parents encouraged Lily to practice social skills, interacting comfortably still felt impossible.

Recognizing that forcing swift personality changes often backfires, Lily's parents took a more empathetic approach by customizing environments around her needs. They transferred Lily to a smaller school with additional emotional support staff trained to nurture hesitant students.

Her new teacher, Ms. Lynn, provided advance notice about what upcoming lessons involved so that Lily could mentally prepare. During group work, Lily was paired with another shy student to collaborate on projects with less pressure to lead vocal conversations.

For recess, Ms. Lynn suggested clubs Lily might enjoy like Art Group rather than noisy competitive games like tag. Making keychains and bookmarks provided natural talking points with like-minded peers. After-school Roblox Club allowed friendships to develop online first.

Seeing Lily thrive in tailored settings focused on her strengths revolutionized her parents' perspective. While still reserved, Lily gained confidence and competence when given the right space to meet her level emotionally. Weekly check-ins with the teacher ensured that the environment continued to help her grow. Compassionately adapting the situations around Lily ultimately transformed her belief in herself.

Secure and Connected

While shy kids crave connection as much as others, their journey getting there follows a less hurried timeline based on their emotional preparedness. Rather than parents and teachers trying to force swift personality shifts, compassionately adapt the situations around shy children to make progress feel secure. Structure breeds confidence. Empower kids to expand their growth socially by creating and promoting a supportive environment, not demanding change alone. Meet them where they are emotionally today by engineering the right conditions for small wins through stage-appropriate challenges and nurturing environments. In time, with our steady guidance surrounding them, shy children will step forward on their own, ready to engage unafraid.

Have faith in the power that environment has to ultimately transform beliefs that your child has in themselves. Your commitment reminds children they deserve to feel safe stepping into situations that are new and uncertain.

Chapter 6:

Specific Communication Strategies to Help Your Child

Smooth, confident communication may not come naturally for reticent kids. However, social connections depend on expressing oneself effectively. The good news is communication abilities can be coached through incremental skill-building tailored to your child's needs. With caring support equipping them to convey thoughts and feelings, the path toward friendship and feeling like they belong opens.

This chapter will explore specific communication strategies that can help shy children navigate social situations. We'll cover conversation starters to initially break the ice, develop acquaintances into deeper friendships over time through vulnerability and care, and cement bonds by being thoughtful friends in return. Communication is the vehicle driving social success. By empowering your child to drive confidence in how they express themselves, they can shift from lonely isolation toward special human connection.

Breaking the Ice

Starting social interactions can feel intimidating for kids who are unsure how to smoothly enter new situations. As a parent, you can empower them with icebreaker tools to ease their way into conversations gently. Provide simple opening lines connected to objects around them to spark friendly small talk.

For example, suggest they compliment a peer's book, game, or sneakers. Then, model incorporating follow-up questions into the banter, like asking about favorite school subjects after a remark on their notebook. Role-play fun exchanges together, such as:

"Cool Pokémon backpack charm! Which Pokémon is your favorite? I like Pikachu."

"Thanks! My favorite is Eevee. What do you like about Pikachu?"

Keep the focus on aligning suggestions with their authentic personality rather than rigid scripts so they can develop a natural style. Equip them with versatile starters and questions for different situations, such as "What's your favorite subject?" or "Which outdoor games do you like?" Rehearse until their delivery sounds natural, not robotic.

Brainstorm ideas spanning different interests they can test out with various peers to see what works best. Refine successful openers and repeat ones that feel right. Collaborate on potential icebreakers like:

"I saw you reading *Dog Man* at lunch—that book looks hilarious!"

"Those Lebron sneakers are awesome! Do you play basketball, too?"

Additionally, co-create play date ideas tailored to their personality, such as baking cookies, playground time, or crafting. Encourage them to invite new friends to preferred activities since they will already feel comfortable and have natural talking points.

Frame invites around making someone's day more fun by including them rather than pressuring them for friendship. Excitement and inclusion are contagious! For example:

"I'm baking chocolate chip cookies after school. Want to come over and decorate some? It'll be super fun!"

Role-play common opening lines to boost their confidence. Take turns kickstarting exchanges until conversations flow more smoothly. Praise all efforts to courageously try new icebreakers with peers, whether successful or not, progress takes practice!

Once your child feels like they have mastered first impression dialogues and phrase templates, collaborate with them on how they can continue those dialogues after introductions. Smooth ice-breaking paves the way for relationship-building over time. Check in on which conversational skills feel harder after the opening sentences so you can jointly brainstorm solutions.

Developing Friendships

Forming close friendships can feel challenging for introverted or shy children. As a parent, you can provide gentle guidance and support tailored to their developmental stage to help them navigate this gradual social process.

Explain to them that having a few meaningful friendships is far more valuable than having a large social circle full of acquaintances. Help them identify a couple of potential close friend prospects from their current peer network that they can focus attention on building a bond with.

In elementary school years, subtly guide them toward classmates who seem to share similar interests or dispositions, by observing kind, compatible behaviors. Gently encourage reciprocal social gestures, like greeting peers, sitting together at story time or lunch, or exchanging notebook doodles, to plant the seeds of friendship. Offer small potential conversation starter scripts they could use, like inviting a classmate to color together during free time. Remind them that real compatibility and common interests are slowly revealed over many months of consistent positive social interactions.

As they transition into older grades, encourage them to nurture moving conversational connections beyond surface-level small talk by sharing likes, telling stories, laughing at jokes, and finding humor in life. Role-play scenarios with your child for initiating potential friendship-building activities, like signing up for a group project, extracurricular activity, or sitting together at the lunch table. When conversational lulls happen, suggest bonding over favorite snacks, toys, books, or characters. Light humor and inside jokes build rapport between emerging connections. Explore each other's identities, dreams, fears, and future goals together.

For pre-teens entering the complex social dynamics that accompany middle school, guide them in identifying values alignment and compatibility subtly by observing how social prospects treat others with kindness and respect. Foster camaraderie through playful banter and inside jokes. Suggest low-risk initial friendship-building activities, like meeting up at a park, bike ride, or trip to get ice cream. Discuss how genuine kindness and compassion cement bonds far more than superficial traits, popularity, or social power. Provide empathetic support and advice when they inevitably encounter social drama. Help them find the confidence to articulate their emotional needs and boundaries to new friends.

By providing developmental stage-specific guidance to map out the nuances of social processes, quiet or shy children can feel empowered to gradually cultivate meaningful mutual bonds with friends over time. Check in sincerely and often about their evolving friend groups at school or in neighborhood friend groups. Offer supportive advice as needed, helping tweak the approach to building friendship bonds with other children. In cases where those bonds aren't working, support them in sharing that it's not anything that they have done, and to continue to say hello and be kind, but to redirect their energy toward reciprocal relationships instead.

Being a Good Friend

Once quiet kids make one or two good new friends, keep coaching them to strengthen bonds through consistent care. Explain step-by-step how to deepen connections week-by-week. Building close friendships takes time and effort on both sides.

Talk about balancing listening and sharing. Teach them to ask their friends lots of questions about likes, feelings, and stories without cutting them off. Show them how to find opportunities to add related things from their own life. Suggest writing down inside jokes or fun memories to repeat later to reinforce bonds. Share fun tales of your childhood friendships so they know that ups and downs are normal.

Practice role plays with them supporting friends through big and small problems. Equip them with caring responses and mature ways to solve conflicts. Remind them no friendship is perfect all the time. Reassure them that bumps along the way won't ruin things if they both want to make up.

Encourage nurturing closeness through keeping promises, making little gifts like cards, or remembering important details. Once it feels right, share something private bit by bit. Remind them that trusting each other completely takes time, not rushing things. They'll soon catch on from examples.

Give them different conversation starters for various cases like events, hobbies, and school topics so they have backup plans when stuck. Have them write down awesome things they notice friends do to repeat later during tough spots. Explore silly jokes bringing everyone laughter when tension needs lifting. Shared giggles heal.

By guiding quiet kids to care about others and speak up for themselves too, you set them up for relationships where they feel safe, understood, and cared for in good and bad times. Check in weekly with them on key friendships to offer helpful, tailored advice.

Managing Social Anxiety

Some children who struggle with social interaction also experience heightened social anxiety in group settings or unfamiliar peer encounters. If you notice frequent signs of nervousness, like avoidance, catastrophic worrying, or physical symptoms when facing potential social engagement, your child may benefit from added guidance to relieve social stress.

To start, validate their worries with empathy rather than dismissing their discomfort. Explain anxiety as a common, manageable human emotion. Share your own childhood shyness stories to normalize their feelings. Discuss that while anxiety feels frightening, it cannot truly harm them long-term.

Provide tools and healthy coping strategies to reduce anxiety, promote self-soothing, and build confidence when facing stressful social triggers. Teach them focused breathing techniques during stressful moments. Help create mantras that challenge negative thinking like "I've got this." Suggest adjusting self-talk from "I'm scared I'll mess up" to "Even if I make a mistake, I can handle it."

Develop pre- and post-event routines that relax. For example, listen to calming music beforehand while envisioning success.

Afterward, write in a journal or talk through how things went. Over time, these routines can reinforce your child's growing capability to handle hard social situations.

With compassionate understanding and several anxiety relief strategies, socially worried kids can develop the courage to move through limiting avoidance toward connection. While social comfort levels and skill-building develop gradually, anxiety management unlocks their confidence one manageable step at a time.

Parent-Teacher Collaboration

Parents lay the groundwork for nurturing communication abilities at home, but children spend considerable time at school navigating verbal interactions with teachers and peers. Collaborating across home and school ensures unified support for a shy child's growth. Let's explore productive ways for parents and teachers to partner on how they can support a shy child in building these skills.

Observe Global Functioning

Parents possess invaluable insights into a child's baseline temperament and communication style patterns in their home environments from an early age. They should then share these foundation notes with teachers so they can gauge student participation more accurately against stable norms. For example, inform the teachers if your child comfortably chats about preferred topics around family but hesitates more among unfamiliar peers.

Likewise, teachers witness students across diverse academic and social situations day to day. Ask them to track observations about your child's overall verbal participation trends and confidence levels when responding to questions, giving presentations, or conversing at recess compared to classmates. Does their demeanor shift when interacting one-on-one or in groups? Request your child's teachers to provide compassionate perspectives in addition to standard academic grades.

Compare Observations

Bring together behavior patterns documented at home and school to determine what the primary triggers and reasons are that your child struggles with some communication, such as busy crowds, unpredictability, criticism, or spotlights. Pinpoint where they shine brightest feeling safe and what specifically overwhelms them. Understanding these different situations better helps you to understand what types of situations allow your child to showcase their strengths more consistently.

Strategize Gradual Steps

Devise gentle incremental communication goals that children feel capable of achieving week-by-week, such as volunteering one remark per book club or asking one question to seek help understanding lessons during class. Agree on realistic expectations that stretch your child's skills without them being paralyzed by perfection. Review and revise approaches based on how your child responds. Remember, don't have the assumption that their progress will be in a straight line—there will be ups and downs and situations of one step forward and two steps back!

Emphasize Assets

Ensure that you have balanced check-in discussions with your child and review their efforts, how they feel, the small wins, as well as any challenges or barriers that they are feeling. For example, celebrate curiosity questions asked privately after class as much as remarks shared aloud in the moment. Honor their preparedness, outlining ideas in writing before presenting orally. Adapt how you measure and judge their communication based on what their challenges are and how they need to improve on and grow in confidence.

Coordinate Touchpoints

Establish consistent family-teacher check-ins via notes, emails, or meetings, briefly reviewing the latest strategies and actions that have been implemented to support your shy child. Solicit your child's input on this, too, so they can talk about what they feel helps them or not. Even five minutes ensures all the different support measures stay thoughtfully aligned to meet the evolving needs of your shy child.

Unified compassion across the places children inhabit daily—home and school—supports their growth immensely. Making collaboration around skill-building a habitual priority, not crisis intervention, sustains shy kids' momentum in conquering their fears long-term until confidence becomes second nature.

Case Study: Sam

Sam was a very shy second grader. He usually only talked if someone spoke to him first. He watched his busy classroom quietly, feeling unseen behind an invisible "glass wall." Approaching new kids felt scary. Group projects made Sam nervous since he struggled to share ideas out loud. He spent most recesses reading alone under a tree.

Seeing Sam's loneliness, his parents provided gentle coaching. They acted out icebreakers together to smoothly join playground games. Sam would ask to play tag or kickball using a script like "That looks fun! Can I join your team?" His parents helped him think of interests he could bond over with classmates, like beloved books, comics, or video games.

As Sam attempted small talk, his parents reminded him making friends takes time, not magic. They helped him notice positive reactions to gauge good friendship fits versus disinterest. Through trial and error, Sam identified two peers more open to his friendship.

Guiding Sam to nurture those potential bonds proved pivotal. His parents suggested taking baby steps in asserting his needs, praising every courageous effort. They role-played patient listening and remembering lots of details when others spoke. For conflicts, they provided empathy scripts promoting kind resolutions.

Fast forward two years: Sam now confidently navigates diverse social situations with a small treasured circle of friends! The communication tools his parents compassionately offered helped Sam find his people and cement bonds after years of silently observing behind glass walls.

Case Study: Clara

Clara is a shy yet imaginative 8-year-old who rarely initiates conversations at school and struggles to maintain friendships. Her creative inner world intimidates her classmates. Group projects overwhelmed Clara, as she froze up when she was expected to collaborate with classmates.

Seeing Clara isolate herself by reading fantasy books rather than playing, her parents gently encouraged her to practice age-appropriate social skills. They role-played icebreakers to smoothly join playground games, like asking "Can I play, too?" After Clara chose science and dragons as interests, they rehearsed how to find common ground conversing about those topics.

As Clara attempted small talk, her parents reminded her that befriending takes time and effort, not instant chemistry. They helped her notice positive social cues like smiling and laughing to identify good friendship potential. Clara eventually grew closer with a fellow bookworm.

Guiding Clara to nurture that bond built confidence. Her parents role-modeled thoughtful listening and validated Clara's challenges by articulating complex thoughts aloud. "Pause, breathe, and speak slowly" became her mantra for calming nerves. Finding their rapport in writing stories together reduced the pressure on Clara to converse for connection with classmates.

While still reserved, Clara can now maintain a small circle of friends with support. Recently, she confidently explained a science experiment to classmates using the communication tools her parents compassionately offered. Their steady guidance helped Clara safely practice the intricacies of friendship at her own introverted pace.

Nurtured Communication

Through compassionate communication guidance, children once trapped behind glass walls observing peers bond without them can now break through to have a meaningful connection with other children. Tailoring strategies to your child's natural personality and developmental stage meets them where they currently are on the spectrum of shyness and anxiety, and then patiently nurtures growth.

Of course, no skill permanently perfects the complex art of friendship. However, equipping children with conversational tools and tips for forging mutual understanding empowers them to confidently chart their course forward in making friends. Remind them that there is no set time frame dictating when they "should" secure relationships. Their courageous efforts today plant seeds blossoming beautifully over time.

Chapter 7:

What Are the Implications for Your Shy Child at School?

Supporting shy, anxious children in navigating school life requires insight, advocacy, and alignment between home and educational environments. Without accommodations and compassionate coaching tailored to their sensitivities, the very settings meant to nurture growth and connection can instead create more distress. However, with proper understanding and support, school can transform from an intimidating arena into a transformative environment that cultivates confidence.

This chapter explores essential strategies for championing your shy child's emotional needs across their pivotal school journey. Whilst we've touched on some actions and strategies linked to the school environment in previous chapters, this particular chapter will be dedicated to the school environment. We'll discuss establishing collaborative partnerships with teachers, speaking up diplomatically for necessary adjustments for your child, achieving cross-environment alignment in care approaches, and gently facilitating social activity participation. With a united commitment to student empowerment school-wide, shy children once paralyzed attending class can overcome that paralysis by gradual exposure until self-confidence takes hold. Let's examine how to make school a platform for helping hesitant students shine.

Building the Right Relationships and Partnerships With School Teachers and Other Staff

Successfully supporting a shy child's emotional needs at school depends on strong collaborative partnerships with teachers and staff. Open ongoing communication channels allow you to share insights equipping them to interpret and nurture your child appropriately. Establishing mutual understanding from the start is crucial for securing supportive care.

1. Schedule meetings before each school year to educate new school staff on your child's temperament, strengths, and sensitivity triggers requiring additional focus. Ask what methods they have successfully used to engage shy students in the past and discuss integrating personalized interventions into routine classroom life. The goal is to set staff up for responsive understanding. Preparing staff ahead of time enables them to understand your shy child and care for them.

2. Request periodic check-ins to exchange updates on how your shy child is doing, both positive and problematic. Monitor potential signs of distress like withdrawal or deterioration. Pay attention to busy schedules when suggesting reasonable check-in frequency. Offer to provide written documentation in between meetings catching teachers up so they can understand any emerging patterns of shy and anxious behavior at home, and review how your shy child is demonstrating them in the school environment. Welcome any input from the school staff's viewpoint to strengthen your strategy. Consistent communication allows both parents and staff to catch issues early before they escalate.

3. Reinforce effective school-family teamwork by sending thank-you notes when teachers go above and beyond in nurturing your child's confidence and connections. Highlight specific examples that classmates noticed. Show grace and empathy when inevitable misunderstandings occur by focusing the next conversations forward on solutions. Any unintentional conflicts between you and the school staff should deepen commitment to collaboration, not derail it. Expressing mutual appreciation solidifies bonds that can weather inevitable bumps as you and the school staff work together to provide the right environment for your shy child to build their confidence.

4. Leverage knowledgeable specialists like school counselors as mediators if needed during clashes. Maintain open, non-defensive dialogue identifying shared goals for your child's growth. Clarify any miscommunications causing upset before proceeding to address significant issues. Reframe conflicts arising from misunderstanding as opportunities for mutual learning. Skillful conflict management prevents deteriorating relationships that would undermine supporting the child, who should be the priority as parents and school staff figure out how to work together to create the right supportive environment.

Laying these responsive foundations ensures shy students receive steady supportive care in this vital development environment from an informed compassionate staff allying with parents. Strengthening bonds between teachers and families leads teachers to transfer greater care to the student. Positive collaboration enables the best outcome: Your child feels understood and encouraged.

Speaking Up and Advocating Your Child's Needs at School

A shy child thriving at school depends on parents and teachers working closely together all year. Building an open, respectful relationship between parents and teachers and sharing observations and information freely will help them learn and make friends. Establishing trust and teamwork between parents and teachers from day one is key to getting them the right support. Start before each new school year and:

- meet with all main teachers to explain your child's special needs simply.

- share their quiet strengths that show up when comfortable and any sensitivity triggers causing stress to your shy child.

- ask what methods worked for engaging shy or anxious students before.

- discuss trying those and other interventions routinely so your child can participate more.

The goal is staff prepared to help proactively. Preparing them ahead enables better care once lessons begin.

Schedule check-ins to exchange updates about how things are going, positive or negative. Provide multiple options for how often meetings work with their calendar. Watch for emotional trouble signs like more silence or academics declining. Request that teachers share observations from the classroom view, too, as issues may emerge there first. Welcome added perspectives to make your support plan stronger. Frequent communication allows catching problems early before there is any escalation that could have been prevented for your shy child.

In between meetings, send quick written updates about relevant things you notice at home, too—social dynamics to navigate, skills to encourage, and small victories unnoticed at school. Offer to provide documentation catching them up so they can track patterns emerging. Keep it simple repeating just enough details for them to link and interpret what they observe in class. Ongoing open information flow is crucial.

When teachers invest extra effort in nurturing your child beyond expectations, reinforce that teamwork. Send thank-you notes each time highlighting any specifics that you learned from your child or classmates. For example, "Bobby said you picked him to lead today's group skit. He felt so proud!" When inevitable mistakes happen, gently refocus the next conversations on potential solutions, not blame. Express authentic appreciation and grace to strengthen bonds and endure bumps.

Get counselors or specialists involved, too, if needed to mediate bigger disagreements or access more support resources. Clearly restate common caring goals for the shy child's growth and development to align perspectives. Then, clarify where communication broke down between the school and parent to address and fix that first. Reframe arguments based on misunderstanding as opportunities to learn rather than damaging important relationships that would undermine the consistent care and support for your child.

Laying this thoughtful open communication foundation ensures extra sensitive students keep getting steady empathetic support at their key learning place from staff unified with their parents. Strengthening teacher-family bonds transfers into warmer care of the child. Smooth collaboration enables the best outcome: Your child feels understood, encouraged, and able to keep improving across environments.

Having Alignment and Agreement on the Strategies to Help Your Child at School and Home

Shy children thrive when the strategies used to bolster their confidence and social skills align across both school and home environments. Collaboration between parents and school staff ensures consistency, which is so important for them to become less anxious. When environments diverge greatly or undermine each other, children receive mixed messages jeopardizing growth. Establishing shared goals, processes, and communication streams helps shy students feel securely understood.

- Discuss with teachers personalized progress goals for your child across academic, emotional, and social domains.

- Agree on indicators for monitoring development and any standard communications procedures when setbacks arise.

- Outline reasonable timelines for staff check-ins on your child's goal progress to exchange insights without overburdening the teacher or parent workloads.

- Plan occasional meetings allowing the child to voice their perspective on how they are feeling they are developing in confidence, across both the school and home environments.

Inform school staff about ongoing tactics being used at home to nurture social confidence so similar approaches can be integrated into their interactions with your child at school. Likewise, learn from them to apply best practices that they have seen in education so you can leverage those consistently in the home environment. Explore potential workshops that can facilitate cross-training opportunities between parents and teachers to strengthen the alignment on how to support your child's shyness and anxiety. Share resources like books, videos, or training links widely to establish foundational knowledge.

Coordinate plans for play dates or special events with peers that support successful social experiences across both settings.

Debrief afterward on observations and what you learned to implement into your support strategy for your shy child. Discuss appropriate friend or activity characteristics that secure your child's comfort, which then allows natural relationships to be built before needing to help orchestrate that for your child. Avoid forcing the intensity, duration, or size of social situations beyond what your child can manage too quickly.

Establish permission protocols giving staff, parents, and trusted specialists access to discussing challenges and victories in supporting your child. Ongoing aligned input from all influential adults in a shy child's life compounds positive effects. Occasionally invite key support players from all parts of your child's life to meetings where as one group you can discuss any ongoing challenges and celebrate incremental wins that might seem minor otherwise.

United understanding together with united action transforms school from an anxiety-provoking arena into a transformative environment cultivating confidence through coordinated care. By synchronizing all the environmental changes in a shy child's life, the adjustments, pace, and communication, you are creating an integrated safety net that supports every attempt towards self-confidence for your shy child. With compassionate unity, shy children brave personal growth.

Encouraging Social Engagements and Activities at School

While shy children often avoid school social functions, gently urging participation in manageable doses expands their comfort zone. Work with staff to engineer encouraging opportunities that suit your child's personality and temperament. Have your child identify which aspects of events normally cause them distress so you can make adjustments to allow for those pain points to be considered. Respect your child's reluctance to get involved while building anticipation of their vital role contributing in their preferred small way. Work with your child's teacher to:

- Suggest roles aligning with temperament like greeting peers, passing out programs, or cleaning up, which allow engagement without spotlight pressures.

- Assign supportive buddies.

- Encourage them to have some smaller responsibilities in these background supporting roles initially before assessing their readiness for more interactive duties over time as their confidence strengthens.

- Offer to remain available during events for encouragement check-ins or to relieve any anxiety that they might feel.

- Discuss providing advance notice about event details like size, noise levels, and duration so they can mentally prepare.

- Allow them to attend portions of larger functions without stigma.

- Praise all efforts.

- Provide quiet rooms for taking short breaks to reset their nervous systems without fully withdrawing from participation.

- After these events, discuss with your child how they feel and what their reactions are. Together, you can identify what alleviated or compounded their discomfort.

- Have them help plan smaller events built around their interests like read-alouds for younger peers, animal care community service, or technology help desks to lower their social hesitation by highlighting competence, ability, and knowledge

- Suggest inviting a close friend to attend together providing familiar peer emotional support. Discuss potential conversation starter strategies, as we covered earlier, associated with activities ahead of time, which will then lower their concern or discomfort before they get involved.

Remind staff that when your shy child avoids activities, it completely reinforces the anxious avoidance cycle. Instead, showing compassionate encouragement fosters empowering new experiences manageable for sensitive dispositions. What first appears smaller, trivial wins or milestones that they meet becomes tremendous growth. Position encouragement as collaboratively removing obstacles to participate rather than pressure without empathy.

With developing insight into your shy child's temperamental needs coupled with using creative ways to make your shy child feel more included, accelerating school connections for reticent students is possible through gradual supportive immersion. Carefully engineered conditions, building up tolerance in progressive steps, can transform interactions that your shy child dreads into confidence-promoting breakthroughs.

Giving Shy Kids Opportunities to Lead

Even quiet kids can become great student leaders with the right support. Start small with roles matching their strengths so it feels less scary. Talk about options like reading to the younger kids, organizing community service projects, or becoming a recess mentor for lonely classmates.

- Explain leadership in simple terms, like making positive change by helping others.

- For first attempts, make detailed plans so they know exactly what to expect. Check in a lot to talk through worries before they grow big. Recruit a teacher mentor to guide bumps along the way. Discuss what parts seem fun versus stressful so you can figure out changes that can make leadership more enjoyable.

- Cheer each tiny, brave step forward even if they stumble, like speaking up or making schedules. Express pride in their effort and care for others, not just the end result. Notice boosts in their confidence after they have tried new things. Save nice compliments from other kids about their work so they remember.

With adult supporters urging them on gently, students once too anxious to raise their hands can grow into leaders who make positive change. Guiding them to find and use their special talents teaches even the shyest kids that their voices and gifts matter in this world. Their quiet influence can spread widely and positively impact others.

How Schools Can Encourage Shy Kids

Schools want all students to join in and learn. However, shy hesitant kids can struggle in loud busy classes. Teachers get stressed trying to push them to talk more. What if schools showed quiet kids that their talents matter instead? Here are easy ways schools can help gentle students come out of their shells. Talk about these with the teachers, and encourage these actions!

Give Advance Notice

Tell shy kids about big projects, plays, or noisy events ahead of time. They feel scared when surprised. Give them prep time to feel more ready. Send notes home to families so they can practice together. Advanced warnings help a lot!

Highlight Their Skills

Every student has special talents. Create projects showing off what sky kids do best—art, writing, computers, helping others. Quiet gifts often go unseen. Show kids that their smart ideas deserve the spotlight sometimes, too! Awards for kindness and creativity make everyone feel celebrated.

Allow Breaks

Loud, wild rooms exhaust timid kids fast. Let them grab noise-blocking headphones, stress balls, or books to take little sensory breaks in chill corners when they need to. Just a few minutes of quiet helps them bounce back. Don't punish resting—it makes participating easier.

Match Buddies

Partner anxious kids with patient peers for group work. Kind friends can model speaking up and pull quiet partners into talking little by little without pressure. Gentle encouragement from classmates their age means a lot! Guide students on how they can support their shy classmates.

Applaud All Progress

Shy kids dread presenting to the full class. But what if they first shared their awesome painting just with the teacher? Or presented their data findings in a video instead of out loud? Applauding baby steps like these makes bigger ones feel possible. Any courage, no matter how small, deserves praise!

Make Participation Options

Not all learning happens through talking nonstop and conversation alone. Let timid kids shine through art, inventions, helping others, or leading small reading groups. There are lots of ways to contribute without having to use a loud bold voice all the time. Playing to strengths makes school feel safe. Different gifts should all be useful.

Involve Families

Ask teachers to tell parents how their caring kid helped a sad classmate or created something beautiful even if they didn't speak up in front of everyone. Families want to know all the ways their child did amazing work. Quiet progress at school matters, too. Send home positive notes.

With simple changes welcoming different personality styles, school becomes a place for gentle ducklings to turn into confident swans gliding ahead. Remove the threats making hesitant kids freeze up. Show them the world needs their gentle care, too. Every child deserves to feel their special gifts belong.

Case Study: May

Since kindergarten, May avoided speaking in class and making friends, instead clinging anxiously to her mother, Laura, during drop-off. Whilst the school was welcoming and a gentle environment, the large elementary school overwhelmed May. She regularly missed class to nurse stomach aches or headaches.

By second grade, after May missed over 20 days that year, Laura requested an evaluation meeting. Gathering the principal, counselor, nurse, and May's teacher, Miss James, Laura explained that May's painful shyness wasn't defiance but disabling anxiety that needed to be addressed and adjusted for.

Laura laid out insights from May's pediatrician and therapist on adjusting school interactions to prevent trigger overstimulation. Miss James had already seated May beside calmer students near the front per Laura's earlier request. The team decided that moving forward, Miss James would provide May with preview materials and progress check-ins during subject and class transitions when possible. The counselor also offered to teach May breathing techniques and set up lunch bunch meet-ups with potential friends.

While still adjusting, with coordinated support, May bravely now participates in class games and plays with girls at recess. Her attendance increased knowing that staff accommodate her sensitivities. Laura expresses gratitude often for their diligent compassion. Though shy, May feels seen, safe, and able to thrive as her best self at school.

Case Study: Ada

Ada is a bright yet very shy 9-year-old who desperately avoids speaking up in her new fourth-grade class. Presenting makes her panic. Though gentle and smart, group work overwhelmed Ada, as she froze up when expected to collaborate. Her frequent absences concerned her parents and teacher.

Seeing Ada isolate herself, her parents requested a meeting with the principal, teacher, and school counselor to create a support plan. They explained Ada's painful shyness stemmed from social anxiety, not defiance. Her pediatrician provided insights on adjusting Ada's school interactions to prevent trigger overstimulation.

Ada's teacher agreed to provide lesson previews and modified how she could participate during intense activities. The counselor offered to equip Ada with discreet cue cards for asking questions that overwhelmed her verbally. Monthly check-ins would help assess progress and tweak supports.

With customized aids in place, Ada slowly strengthened her confidence in contributing to class and connecting with peers. Her parents and teacher also aligned strategies at home to further reinforce growth. Celebrating each brave step forward, no matter how small, became vital.

While still adjusting, Ada can now participate in some group work, thanks to compassionate coordination between staff and parents prioritizing her emotional needs equally to her academic needs. Nurturing an environment where Ada felt heard allowed her strengths and victories to emerge. Consistent encouragement surrounding Ada ultimately helped her to believe in herself.

Opportunities Abound

Shaping school into a growth-enabling environment for shy, anxious children requires ongoing teamwork, advocacy, and creativity in providing emotional support. However, the rewards for establishing compassionate systems backing students as they stretch beyond paralyzing discomfort are immense. Gradually, with united encouragement surrounding them, once hesitant children take proud steps forward socially, uncovering confidence they didn't know was already them.

The strategies in this chapter equip parents and staff to champion the shy child's journey with insight and care. This transformation reaches beyond the individual to impact school communities now positioned to nurture all students' belonging and not just the outwardly extroverted. When environments affirm the strengths of different sensitivities and personalities, new educational paradigms emerge where differences are celebrated, not constrained. Helping shy students blossom ripples outward to touch us all.

Chapter 8:

How Technology, Digitization, and Social Media Is Impacting Shy Children

As childhood rapidly digitizes, technology's double-edged sword uniquely impacts shy youth. Immersive screens and networks can either exacerbate isolation by replacing vital in-person relationship-building or facilitate connections that were unimaginable before. Our guidance in navigating this complex landscape is essential so digital life supplements rather than sabotages a child's social development.

This chapter explores practical strategies to harness technology's power while protecting emotional vulnerability. We'll cover optimizing social media for bonding within limits, mentoring digital etiquette and ethics, cooperative screen time boundaries, and monitored online interactions. While the elimination of all potential risks is impossible, responsible guidance aligned with your child's temperament can transform devices from an obstacle to an opportunity promoting confidence.

The Impact of Technology on Social Development

Technology plays an increasingly central role in childhood social development, with complex implications for shy children. Thoughtful monitoring and mentoring are crucial to ensure technology helps rather than hinders social skill-building. Digital immersion can provide connections but should complement rather than replace vital in-person relationships. Ongoing age-appropriate guidance helps shy kids reap benefits while avoiding pitfalls.

Technology overuse can limit in-person interactions essential for friendship development. But sites connecting youth over shared interests can also help shy children find peers, which can ease their social immersion into different groups. Moderated online gaming communities can support joint play and teamwork talk that might be missed on isolated playgrounds. This allows children to use technology to inspire real-world friendships through shared passions, not prevent them. Having a good balance of screen time with other enriching activities is important for the well-being of all children.

If face-to-face attempts at conversations feel intimidating, video calls can be good for your shy child to practice visual conversation cues in lower-pressure settings. Yet screen over-reliance risks stunting capacities to read real-time social dynamics and emotional nuances. Balance is key. Allow devices to build skills that should be gradually done face-to-face as confidence strengthens, but limit technology usage to avoid your child using tech as a replacement for developing essential skills for growth.

Without guidance, shy kids may use devices to avoid social anxiety rather than build competence through manageable exposures. Discuss balancing activities and model healthy technology habits yourself as adults. Apps promising social salvation should spark conversation about underlying emotions, not replace human support. Gently curb tech overuse as an anxiety avoidance tactic. Redirect your shy child to coping strategies and real-world interactions to help increase their confidence and comfort levels.

Monitor digital etiquette and oversharing personal information and feelings online. Role-play with your child on how to express needs or navigate conflict through tech-mediated communication when appropriate. Our task is steering our children toward tools and strategies to support building their confidence and not substituting their lack of confidence with technology. Mentorship molds healthy usage. Install parental controls and directly discuss online safety, given shy kids' higher risk levels of following others when feeling digitally pressured. Peer victimization hides more easily behind screens.

Monitoring Online Interactions

Vigilantly monitoring shy children's online interactions helps ensure tech supports rather than sabotages social skill-building. Gently observe your child's usage to guide appropriate use that minimizes any risks to building their self-esteem. Allow them to have some privacy, but discuss how technology can exploit everyone, including adults, redirecting them toward safe and ethical digital conduct. Help them self-identify different online communities that elicit authentic self-expression, not mask through false personas.

Track social media connections, prioritizing depth over quantity and their emotional impact. Help shy kids learn signs of real friendship that are compatible with where they are in growing their confidence. Kindly discuss removing toxic people or connections they have met through technology. Guide your children in how to recognize when social courage might be misplaced online with ulterior or malicious motives. Remind them that slow friendships developed online can create meaningful bonds, too.

Discreetly scan chat group dynamics assessing who is included in them. Redirect your child away from communities tolerating victimization or inappropriate content. Have ongoing discussions about seeking versus providing support online. Demonstrate how you can conduct yourself and support others by conducting yourself ethically when witnessing marginalization, neither joining in nor being complicit. Remind your child that home is a non-judgmental space for learning how to use technology and navigate complicated digital experiences.

For young children, directly co-view and co-play games, videos, and multiplayer worlds, assessing their safety and monitoring their chats. Maintain parental controls that filter the content your child is exposed to and ensure that it matches their maturity. Prevent social modeling by avatars using language or behavior that you wouldn't permit in person. Pause play to discuss confusing interactions and demonstrate how they can work through certain situations in an empathetic way.

Model proactively addressing digital drama and oversharing rather than avoiding discomfort. Our calm oversight of our child's technology and digital usage builds confidence in how they handle techno-social challenges independently as they get older, through increasing exposure that we support. Openly discuss your own past age-appropriate encounters maturing into wiser digital media use to reassure trial-and-error learning. Nothing is straightforward, and there will be trial and error with your child as you both find a comfortable way of managing this!

While sheltering shy children online is tempting, measured steps into supervised digital usage teach skills that eventually navigate independent online connections. Give your child space to retreat when needed, but encourage them to increase their usage and confidence in using technology. Technology is here to stay and is unavoidable! Even shy adults depend on some digital fluency.

Setting Screen Time Limits (and the Tough Conversations That Go Along With It)

Limiting shy children's recreational screen time is essential yet often elicits resistance. Compassionately convey limits emphasizing real-world in-person social connections that technology overuse could hinder. Call a family meeting to collaboratively establish guidelines for balancing device use with in-person activities and responsibilities. Compromise gives them autonomy within structured boundaries. Consider tying usage to completing responsibilities or directly replacing online engagements with alternate enriching activities. Make clear how success is defined, whether screen time or achieved activities, rather than policing it in a punitive manner.

Preface putting tougher restrictions in place by explaining how excessive immersion can stall the development of vital social skills and management of anxiety. Highlight positive real-world alternative activities that can align with their interests. Guide your child in discovering offline passions that could become careers or community contributions matching their innate skills. Help envision a life of purpose possible beyond screens.

When technology limits are inevitably challenged by your child, use it as an opportunity to probe their objections more deeply to identify and address root frustrations or disappointments they now feel an online environment can fix for them. Guide expressing emotions productively. Offer focused one-on-one time and undivided listening to counter the loss of connection that tech overuse often compensates for.

Set your own modeling examples by minimizing phone fixation during shared family time. Install lock-out apps preventing late-night social media usage that can sabotage sleep, which is essential to help with positive mood and judgment. Make device charging stations public spaces rather than private bedrooms to discourage tech-enabled isolation.

While shy children often fiercely defend screen preoccupations, limits with empathy ultimately teach healthier dependence on devices, not the elimination of this intrinsic modern reality. Moderation is achievable. With collaborative enforcement of balanced usage, the risks posed by excessive immersion transform into age-appropriate monitored opportunities promoting confidence.

Digital Etiquette and Safety

Guiding shy children to interact online safely and ethically protects them from increased risks that their vulnerability poses virtually.

- Tailor ongoing age-appropriate digital citizenship lessons.

- Establish clear rules for information sharing, gaming communications, and seeking friends online.

- Educate your child on precautions like avoiding identity disclosure, enabling privacy settings, recognizing scams/spam, and the permanence of web content.

- Discuss your responsibility to guide them in preventing avoidable harm in this complex landscape, not punish inevitable mistakes as they continue to learn and develop their judgment.

- Outline your expectations and accountability procedures should they fail to follow safety rules.

- Welcome any questions that they have to ease their confusion and make sure they understand the role you have in keeping them safe and helping them understand the benefits and risks of technology.

- Train them to identify useful and positive versus toxic online spaces and seek your guidance in reporting any encountered threats, cyberbullying, or inappropriate content.

- Rehearse with your child how they can confidently respond to digital peer pressure by refusing unsafe requests.

- Praise your child for coming to you with any questions even if they are embarrassed. This shows that they are developing confidence, maturity, and trust.

- Ask guiding questions to help them understand the technology space instead of punishing them for situations that they still don't understand when using technology.

- Discuss the ethics of screen time usage, avoiding deception about usage, respecting digital consultations, and proper citation of online content.

- Explore case studies that prompt questions about the ethics of complex issues like privacy, censorship, copyright, hacking, AI, and workplace automation all affected by technologies. It doesn't matter whether your child is only 6 or even younger, you can still start to foster their understanding of balancing free online speech with avoiding harm.

- Install parental control software that appropriately restricts access to mature platforms and monitors concerning search terms. Also openly discuss sexuality safety given that there is an escalated risk online for exploitation or shame. Your oversight of your child's use of technology aims to empower them to make ethical informed independent decisions about risks that come with the freedom of adulthood in due time and not to indefinitely control everything that they are doing.

Equipping shy youth to practice core values online ultimately provides transferable skills in navigating the benefits and hazards of increasing their technological usage as digital citizens. Just as social competence strengthens slowly offline through modeling and mentorship, so too should we shepherd virtual development age-appropriately. Progress in how a shy child can appropriately leverage technology to manage their confidence and anxiety will be faster with the right support in place at home and school.

Promoting Healthy Gaming for Shy Kids

Video games provide opportunities for shy children to socialize and build confidence in the digital realm. Games featuring chatting or playing in teams require communication cooperation and collaboration toward common goals. It allows them to practice with peers and potential new friends from the comfort of home. Parental oversight ensures gaming supplements rather than replaces vital offline social development. To help promote healthy gaming for your child:

- Monitor your child's emotional state before and after gaming sessions to ensure that their moods remain healthy.

- Set time limits on daily gaming by balancing screen time with other activities.

- Guide children to self-regulate when they become overstimulated or frustrated.

- Teach techniques such as taking deep breaths, sitting quietly, or using a fidget toy to soothe emotions.

- Provide a designated quiet space for children to retreat to independently when they need to re-center.

- Equip kids with reassuring self-talk phrases like "I've got this" or "I am calm."

- Model self-care strategies in challenging moments so they learn to show themselves compassion.

- Build these simple skills early on so children can deploy self-regulation strategies automatically as needed.

- Research age-appropriate games featuring chat functions with other players.

- Supervise initial sessions by assessing the safety, civility, and age-appropriateness of the language used in the games.

- Praise attempts your child makes in interacting online, such as assisting teammates, and demonstrate to them how they can exit any toxic conversations.

- Help them understand which connections are authentic versus impersonal.

- Discuss examples of good sportsmanship and being a respectful teammate.

- Explain that gaming requires patience, and losing is an opportunity to improve.

- Offer to play together to practice useful communication techniques for specific situations.

Monitor your child's emotional state before and after gaming sessions to ensure that their moods remain healthy. Set time limits on daily gaming by balancing screen time with other activities. Guide children to self-regulate when they become overstimulated or frustrated. Teach techniques such as taking deep breaths, sitting quietly, or using a fidget toy to soothe emotions. Provide a designated quiet space for children to retreat to independently when they need to re-center. Equip kids with reassuring self-talk phrases like "I've got this" or "I am calm." Model self-care strategies in challenging moments so they learn to show themselves compassion. Build these simple skills early on so children can deploy self-regulation strategies automatically as needed.

Research age-appropriate games featuring chat functions with other players. Supervise initial sessions by assessing the safety, civility, and age-appropriateness of the language used in the games. Praise attempts your child makes in interacting online, such as assisting teammates, and demonstrate to them how they can exit any toxic conversations. Help them to understand which connections are authentic versus impersonal. Discuss examples of good sportsmanship and being a respectful teammate. Explain that gaming requires patience, and losing is an opportunity to improve. Offer to play together to practice useful communication techniques for specific situations.

For young kids, choose educational multiplayer games that build vocabulary and math skills collaboratively. Monitor the games to ensure that there is positive social modeling rather than uncontrolled chatter. Ask about new friends made and facilitate introducing gaming buddies to each other for cooperative offline play dates. Set expectations for polite language and take turns speaking and listening. Have them recap what they learned by playing educational games. Intervene if you observe inappropriate speech or behavior from either your child or others that they are playing with online.

Share your own age-appropriate gaming interests playing together. Model skills such as introducing yourself, taking turns, apologizing for mistakes, and consideration for all players. Discuss examples of feedback that was helpful versus unconstructive to your child. Highlight how you have seen them develop and improve in their collaboration, problem-solving, and communication over time through gaming. Explore non-violent family games that emphasize teamwork. Talk about each family member's gaming strengths. Establish device-free family game nights.

Additionally, interested older kids can research streaming platforms that allow broadcasting gameplay and commentary to followers. Supervise initial streams by assessing safety and the emotional impact of public commentary. Prepare them for any negativity that may arise while empowering them to block abusive viewers. Celebrate the emotional resilience that they show if this happens. Agree with your children about online safety and etiquette rules before they do any streaming. Check in on their comfort level with public posting. Remind them that their self-worth shouldn't depend on the approval of strangers.

Guiding their gaming experiences teaches shy children social cues, ethics, and skill-building that can also apply to offline relationships. By carefully expanding their comfort zones digitally first, confidence in socially navigating wider worlds emerges over time.

Promoting Healthy Social Media Habits

Social media plays an increasingly pivotal role in childhood socialization, with unique implications for shy youth. Thoughtful guidance helps ensure platforms supplement confidence rather than sabotage it. Let's explore healthy social media mentoring strategies that promote skill-building within wise boundaries.

Discuss Online Identity Mindfully

Guide shy kids interacting online through the lens of their best inner self; that is to say, encourage them to be authentic and themselves. Brainstorm profile handles and images that reflect genuine interests and strengths rather than flashy facades attempting to impress others. Share your own thought process on how you created an authentic social media presence versus false personas. Model self-acceptance offline transitioning to healthy self-expression online.

Set Private Accounts

Restrict connections to existing friends and family by enabling private settings. Review your child's contact lists and online visibility options together. Explain that securing personal information protects privacy and personal safety. Explore any platform tools that help with managing connections, blocking bullies, and filtering inappropriate content. Demonstrate how to report abusive behavior. Ensure that the setting remains locked down during these key developmental stages of your child's life. The complexity of how to manage social connections online often is more difficult to manage than the maturity of your child allows.

Encourage Bond-Building Platforms

Suggest youth-oriented platforms known for shared interests like art, causes, gaming, or creators. This is better than sharing photos that can potentially damage through superficial judgment. Guide your child in discovering subgroups that resonate with their unique personality. Ask about new friends that they have found and made and take the focus away from how many "followers" they have. Discuss meaningful examples of support or common values that can make virtual friendships stronger. Create an environment where the depth of a new friendship is more important than having a lot of followers or connections.

Monitor Balance

Discreetly observe social media usage to ensure it supplements vital offline friendships and interests rather than substituting for them. Take note of any complaints that your child makes about FOMO (fear of missing out). Take time to discuss any unhealthy comparisons your child makes with their peers that are creating distress for them. Identify when they are over-using technology to escape from real-life worries. Help establish online connection objectives, then set collaborative limits and device-free bonding activities. Gently redirect excessive usage of technology that can then sabotage your child's overall well-being.

Address Online Drama Compassionately

When digital social turmoil inevitably occurs, avoid shaming your child while addressing the issues and applying any specific restrictions. Teach kids to block, report, or log off rather than counter-attack. Use any missteps to talk about accountability and any mistakes that your child makes with technology to proactively discuss amends if they have caused any harm or offense. Probe any underlying behaviors that you observe your child manifesting online like insecurity or impulse control. Guide your child in making specific and thought-out choices online, instead of reactive ones.

Coach Confident Self-Expression

Shy kids require extra support when they are learning to healthily self-advocate online. Offer them scripts of specific phrases that they can use calling out mistreatment or standing up for diversity with others online. Review draft posts that they want to share online to mentor assertive captions championing neglected communities or sharing vulnerability. Reiterate to your child that it is powerful to be honest and speak the truth whilst balancing that with not taking risks online. Foster moral courage in expressing identity online.

By bringing together discipline with compassionate mentoring of social media literacy, we can support healthy usage of this as kids find their digital voice. Guiding them in this now lets them develop habits so they can gain the confidence to enjoy and benefit from social media and the inevitable technologies influencing society ahead.

Case Study: Grace

Grace is a shy 11-year-old who loves posting her anime art online but struggles with mean comments. Though talented, she anxiously deletes her posts when people criticize her art. She also compulsively checks notifications, losing sleep and falling behind on schoolwork.

Seeing Grace grow reliant on external validation, her parents Nina and Andre intervened with compassion. They openly discussed concerns about social media impacting Grace's self-confidence and distracting her from also focusing on the in-person interactions in her life.

Together, they instituted screen time limits on shallow social sites while still allowing Grace access to art channels valuing substance over followers. Finding in-person anime friends through events reduced her reliance on fickle and sometimes mean online connections. Modeling self-care, Nina role-played responding to cruel remarks by blocking bullies and reminding Grace of how she should have confidence in herself and her art.

While Grace still requires support managing screen habits, her parents' guidance helped her to realize self-worth can't come from strangers' approval. Nina continues collaborating on digital etiquette and redirecting her use of this towards constructive connections suiting Grace's introversion. With compassion, not control, she steers Grace safely through virtual worlds awaiting her generation.

The Next Generation

Technology will shape rising generations' social realities in ways we are still trying to understand, and that are ever-changing. But our steady support can prepare shy youth to skillfully balance virtual connectivity with genuine intimacy as digital natives. What seems risky terrain given our children's sometimes sensitive and shy personalities today merely paves the way for pioneering greater access, community, and well-being online tomorrow.

With compassion and wisdom, not fear, we can guide children into safe digital spaces eliciting self-confidence while also knowing when to unplug. As parents and caregivers, we should help our children interpret how to best use and enjoy technology rather than trying to police and punish with the constant technological shifts and advancements. Where overprotection leaves youth naively vulnerable, empathy and accountability will allow them to have competent digital citizenship, helping shy kids gain confidence in controlling their devices rather than being controlled by them.

Chapter 9:
Cultivating Quiet Superpowers

While shy children face some unique social challenges, their innate sensitivities also harbor invaluable gifts. Through parents' and teachers' guidance in nurturing introverted talents, what initially seems like weakness can transform into an explosion of empathy, creativity, resilience, and leadership changing the world for the better.

This chapter explores ways parents can reveal incredible strengths hiding within shy children by mentoring emotional and creative intelligence suited especially to their disposition. We'll highlight role model innovators and trailblazers who once felt socially paralyzed themselves, before pioneering global change. Our children's so-called "weaknesses" frequently form the foundation of their superpowers when properly understood and supported.

Empathy and Emotional Intelligence

Shy kids notice subtle emotional shifts and unspoken suffering in others that their more extroverted peers may not, thanks to their natural perception and sensitivity to others. Help them recognize how this special ability to read people can be used powerfully in careers like psychology, counseling, teaching, medicine, and creative arts, where they can leverage their unique emotional intelligence. Discuss ways that they might shape more societies to someday be more compassionate and understanding of shyness and social anxiety. Their sensitivities and experiences with this hold them in good stead to influence and help others with this in the future.

Role model how to stand up to exclusion, judgment, or marginalization of others politely yet courageously when they witness this, even if speaking out feels terrifying. Demonstrate how calling out these injustices or showing vulnerable peers simple kindnesses makes positive ripples that can have a longer-term positive impact on culture and societies. They will be relying on the very thing that has challenged them (a lack of confidence) to use for the power of the greater good.

Highlight activists, philosophers, and writers such as Susan Cain, Mahatma Gandhi, and Florence Nightingale who leveraged empathy and ethics (over loud charisma) and created major positive social shifts to challenge conformity and norms of their age. How might your child lead quiet revolutions someday themselves?

Creativity and Innovation

The rich inner life that shy children cultivate through solitary activities like reading, journaling, art, and independent projects can fuel outside-the-box, sometimes genius, ideas. Help them appreciate how creativity works best with substantial quiet thinking time fully developing ideas—a built-in strength for introspective temperaments. They may feel bored or scared that they are missing out on other activities or things their peers are doing. However, time spent on solitary activities won't be wasted and could be the beginning of amazing things to come. Amazing works are coming when ready!

Encourage writing stories, comic books, poems, or original songs so they are independently creating and imagining these things without the pressure to share before anything is ready to share. More opportunities to showcase these creations more publicly will come when they are ready and the time is right. For now, focus on the process of creating lots of ideas and not critically evaluating them. Attribution science confirms that a person's creativity largely depends not necessarily on their natural gifts but instead on the number of ideas someone has over the years. Building those habits now allows shy kids' ideas to slowly percolate into works that change thinking.

Highlight innovators such as J. K. Rowling, Emily Dickinson, and Ludwig van Beethoven, who overcame significant social adversity through the unconventional power of creatively channeling their shyness and sensitivity and producing pieces of work that have changed societies. The world needs every type of mindset spurring inspiration in their own timing creating work at their own pace.

Build passion projects like apps, animation, jewelry design, or architecture model construction suited to your child's technical and artistic strengths. These constructive solo pursuits teach tangible competencies applicable to collaborative academic and career environments down the road. By learning and doing these types of activities on their own, they become innovative leaders, confident communicators, and experts on topics they care about who add much-needed diversity to teams and society. Pursuing genuine interests now cultivates skills that are transferable to passionate vocations improving society tomorrow by adding their unique voice.

Quiet Leadership Strengths

Shy kids often prefer working behind the scenes, but their kindness, good listening, and patience can make them great leaders. Ask them to describe their favorite teachers or coaches so they might recognize some similar strengths or characteristics within themselves. Talk to your shy kid about how nervousness can also be considered as thoughtfulness and care. They can start small, leading service projects, camp songs, or family chores.

Discuss future jobs using these talents, such as teaching, counseling, medicine, research, and activism. Find causes for your shy kids that match their passions. Show heroes such as Mahatma Gandhi and Temple Grandin, who led quietly with compassion and conviction, not loud bossing. Show your children that their gentle courage can influence others when they are ready. Guide them to recognize everyday leaders around them who are creating change step-by-step. Teach them that their influence starts small.

Resilience and Mental Toughness

Facing early social bumps builds lifelong resilience when you help your child handle it calmly, like calming their worries, keeping hope alive, and resolving arguments kindly. Gently praise your child each time they push past their discomfort or solve conflicts peacefully. Have them journal the moments that they felt proudest by persevering despite there being challenges.

Share stories about people who stood up against bullies, including inventors Newton and Darwin or writer Harper Lee. Discuss how sticking to their visions ultimately shifted how societies and communities thought, even though they had to deal with criticism and loneliness first. Frame their journey with optimism.

Self-Aware Identities

Shy kids' high self-awareness helps them stay true to their personality, not to the pressure to be popular. Urge them to explore through journaling and discussing what they care about most. Who do they hope to become someday?

Guide them to identify within themselves what makes them unique as their characters continue to develop. The sensitivity in shy children can be seen as wisdom and not weakness. Reflection reveals the truth. Embracing their real selves positions happiness over chasing the approval of other people around them. Their temperament already contains special gifts, if they listen quietly within.

Leveraging Sensitivity as a Leadership Strength

While shyness can feel socially limiting, the same sensitive perceptiveness, care for others, and rich inner life that characterizes introverted children also harbor incredible leadership talents that can change the world. Let's explore ways to reframe "weaknesses" as strengths that can build confidence and purpose.

Noticing Unmet Needs

Shy kids who are sensitive to suffering may spot overlooked injustices and unsolved problems more readily than their outwardly focused peers. Help your child appreciate how sensitivity is a prerequisite for improving society. Their similar situations put them in a unique position to help improve the status quo. Discuss this with them and consider where they might make a difference, starting with, for example, what they might observe as an injustice at school.

Leading Through Listening

The patience and care that shy kids demonstrate enable them to lead powerfully through compassionate listening, not top-down instructions or orders. They may absorb diverse perspectives before considering what the implications of these are. There could be opportunities for them to do such things as lead small groups emphasizing emotional support like camp counselors, peer mentors, or reading buddies. Highlight examples of introverted icons such as Rosa Parks, whose quiet backbone strengthened communities.

Persisting Toward Purpose

Spotlight activists, writers, and scientists who faced adversity like bullying but persisted privately and developed unconventional ideas that helped humankind. Discuss how staying true to one's conscience and talents in the face of external criticism requires incredible resilience. Help them align interests like robotics or poetry with potential real-world problems that need innovative solutions. Reframe sensitivity as a strength that can lead to resilience and persistence and ultimately make the world a better place!

Centering Ethics and Inclusion

Role model standing up to exclusion and judgment with empathy and not aggression. Demonstrate to your child how to advocate respectfully for someone left out of games or conversations. Discuss historical figures who peacefully unified communities by promoting justice and diversity. Nurture your child's natural courage by speaking out when they see someone being mean, and by also teaching them to forgive gracefully. Emotional intelligence applied ethically makes great leaders.

Supporting Behind the Scenes

Not all leadership means being visible as the leader. Very often leaders are quietly driving change behind the scenes through diligent organizing, uplifting morale, and logistics. Help shy kids recognize and employ talents like preparation, active listening, and project coordination making collaboration possible. Every role holds equal importance for progress.

With insight and encouragement, we can reveal incredible influencers already growing within our sensitive youth. The "weaknesses" forcing them to retreat socially actually contain underdeveloped strengths which one day could make society a better place. It's our job to carefully cultivate empathy, ethics, and resilience into a force for good.

Case Study: Rico

Rico is a caring yet very shy 12-year-old who overcomes his social anxiety to stand up for marginalized peers at school. Though admirably courageous, Rico downplays acts like welcoming new students or reporting bullies privately to teachers as "not a big deal." He discounts profound kindness as ordinary, reflecting his intrinsically high emotional intelligence.

Noticing Rico hiding his light under a bushel, his parents intervened to highlight special perceptiveness and moral leadership that quietly empowers positive change. They connected empathy fueling his social advocacy to careers in counseling, teaching, or medicine someday. Discussing society's urgent need for more defenders of empathy like Mahatma Gandhi and Florence Nightingale reinforced how important it is for him to confront injustice, even though, at times, it felt terrifying to speak up.

Rico's parents made time with him to discuss emotional dynamics and ethical dilemmas his maturity sensitively picks up on that many of his peers didn't notice, modeling how to gracefully respond. They highlighted his maturity and identifying with others' suffering as hard-won strengths arising from his own adversity. Eventually feeling understood then allowed Rico to embrace standing up through ethical care-giving as his superpower. Rico does this at his own pace when he feels confident enough to speak up, no matter how small he might think the situation is.

Rico knows that he has a very compassionate support system that has helped him work on increasing his confidence and also positively nurturing his emotional strength. This confidence enables him to prioritize moral speaking up instead of following the crowd. By nurturing Rico's introverted talents early, his parents showed him a possible future that leverages his sensitivity and resilience.

Case Study: Nora

Nora is a shy 10-year-old who finds refuge in writing imaginative short stories. Though remarkably talented, she resists sharing her pieces with anyone, even family, out of fear they might not appreciate her offbeat style. Nora avoids writing clubs as she feels too exposed to peers. She worries that because she is so sensitive, this will limit her confidence and her future success.

Seeing Nora discount her gift, her parents compassionately intervened to shift her mindset about this. They helped her recognize highly inventive thinkers who often require quiet time to develop their visions privately, before sharing them publicly. Her parents showed examples of where they had shared their first attempts at things such as paintings before they had developed more skills with them. This comforted Nora realizing nearly all pioneering artists across history required extensive solo exploration, creating multiple versions of their work, long before they achieved fame.

Her parents highlighted innovators like Ludwig Van Beethoven and Emily Dickinson who overcame similar social adversity and channeled working in isolation into creating famous music and writing. Nora felt understood, not rushed. They encouraged her authentic writing voice without critique, focusing on her enjoying it before evaluating it. Freedom to cultivate imagination and a growth mindset helped Nora gain confidence in her quiet calling.

Recently, Nora decided submitting a story to a youth writing contest could be a small courageous step. She may not win awards tomorrow but now trusts her lifelong love affair crafting new worlds through her writing to continue to build her expertise. Nora's parents believe in the incredible author and that she already is flourishing one gentle page at a time.

Gifts Abound

In the end, the emotional and creative gifts shy children develop to manage anxiety and isolation become the very superpowers that can make wide positive change when given the right direction and support.

Rather than viewing their sensitivity as a weakness, guide your children to appreciate how staying true to themself and their individuality can create a society where all members feel valued. Your shy children's role as observers and empathizers is absolutely essential in society. Continue to demonstrate to them how emotional intelligence builds rapport and relationships that are equally or more valuable in the long term than charisma. You can model that standing up for themselves and others through culture, ethics, and courage against cruelties is what is needed for communities and societies to continue to progress.

In time, shy or socially anxious children realize that their destiny never entailed "overcoming" shyness because their destiny is perfect for who they actually are—sensitive thinkers who can improve the world through empathy and creativity, compassion and resilience that have been strengthened by adversity. With the encouragement to recognize the quiet powers within them, shy kids gain confidence that their contributions hold profound importance exactly as they are.

Chapter 10:

Challenges and How to Manage Them

Supporting a shy child in building lifelong confidence and self-esteem comes with both triumphs and challenges. As a parent, you'll celebrate breakthrough moments when your child takes social risks, finds their voice, and understands and accepts their self-worth. Yet there will also be setbacks, meltdowns, and external factors threatening to unravel the progress. This chapter addresses the realities all parents face—the ups, downs, and tools needed to nurture confident and resilient children in the long run.

When your child struggles with new social situations or goes backward after trying something new, don't lose hope. Their development will happen in a two steps forward, one step back fashion rather than a straight path upward. Along the way, equip your child with coping strategies for handling problems independently and self-soothing anxiety. Help them foster a growth mindset that celebrates effort over outcome. Recognize when professional support may provide added guidance tailored to your child's needs. As with most lifelong skills, confidence ebbs and flows; but with consistent love, sharing examples, and belief in your child's inner strengths, they will continue blossoming self-assuredly into the person they're meant to become.

Setbacks Are Part of the Process

It can be frustrating when you've worked hard to implement strategies from this book, but your shy child still struggles with confidence and self-esteem. Know that setbacks are an expected part of the process. Not every strategy will work perfectly or instantly improve things. Children often take two steps forward and one step back as growth happens gradually, especially with building lifelong skills like self-confidence. Have realistic expectations when trying new techniques with them and don't expect overnight changes. Be compassionate with yourself as a parent trying hard to help your child in this journey. Shift your mindset to view stumbles as opportunities to adjust your approach to how to help your child

When you hit roadblocks, don't view them as failures. Reframe setbacks as an opportunity to try something new or adjust your approach. Review the challenges your child is facing and brainstorm tweaks to strategies or ideas for alternatives. Is there an underlying concern that needs to be addressed first? Do smaller, more incremental goals need to be set? Does the strategy need to be tailored to your child's interests? Don't forget to celebrate small wins and milestones along the way. Track what is helping versus what is hindering progress with the actions that you are putting in place to help your child become more confident. Consult peers, teachers, or professionals for an outside perspective if you feel stuck at any time. And don't forget that you might have some friends in your network who are experiencing something similar with their children. Share experiences and learn from each other!

Keep lines of communication open and regularly speak with your child about how they are feeling. Check in with them about what's working versus what's challenging for them. Actively listen without judgment. Make it safe for your child to share their perspective so you can better guide and support them. Model vulnerability by sharing your own struggles and self-doubt. Help reframe "failures" into lessons learned.

Remain calm and thoughtful if your child gets upset or discouraged.

Ups and downs are part of progress when gaining confidence. Over time, shy children will get better at self-soothing, overcoming nerves in social situations, taking risks like public speaking, and building resilience no matter the outcome when trying new things. Stay patient, flexible, and encouraging with both your child and yourself. You've got this, even during the difficult times. Praise effort and courage, not just success. Lean on other parents for solidarity during the ups and downs. Trust that you and your child have all the inner strength needed to get through the challenges.

Role of Resilience

Supporting a shy child in building confidence and self-esteem takes resilience from both the parent and the child. As a parent, you must model resilience in the face of setbacks, disappointments, judgment from others, and your child's ups and downs. Your ability to bounce back gives your child permission to do the same. Demonstrate that mistakes are learning opportunities, not reasons to quit. Show your child that persistence in the face of challenges is what leads to growth. Praise effort and courage, not just outward success. Don't forget to offer empathy and comfort when your child is struggling before encouraging them to try again. Focus on progress and self-improvement rather than comparing them to others. Remain calm and steady in your support regardless of external circumstances.

Similarly, shy children need to build their resilience muscle to gain confidence over time. They will face fears, anxiety, bullying, failures, and other difficulties. Help them to reframe struggles as opportunities to practice resilience that will serve them throughout life. Teach them strategies such as positive self-talk, taking breaks when frustrated, or asking for help.

Share stories of when you felt shy or demoralized but didn't give up. The more children tap into their inner resilience, the greater their self-belief becomes. In your own life (using age-appropriate examples) demonstrate your resilience strategies by talking through them aloud as you implement them. This will help your child see how you continue even when things seem difficult.

Harnessing the Power of "Yet"

Use visual reminders such as growth mindset posters about the power of "yet." The power of yet refers to the growth mindset concept that just because a child cannot do something now does not mean they will never be able to do it. The word "yet" signifies further potential and future capability. For example, if a child says, "I can't ride a bike," an adult can respond with "You can't ride a bike *yet*." This emphasizes that while the child cannot currently ride a bike, they have the power to learn and succeed in the future.

Using these visual reminders serves as an ongoing motivation and reflection for children that their capabilities continue to expand. When they see the poster about the power of yet, it reinforces that difficulties and struggles are part of the learning process rather than a dead end. It inspires persistence to keep trying and conveys the belief that they can and will continue to grow. The reminders are a simple way to instill the mindset that children's abilities are not fixed but, rather, can progress significantly through practice over time. Ultimately, it is about highlighting their potential by focusing on "yet" instead of "can't."

Replenishing Your Resilience

On difficult days, take a breather to replenish your own resilience. Turn to supportive friends, a therapist, or rejuvenating activities. You can't support others and encourage them if you aren't taking care of your own mental and physical health. Make time for exercise, nutrition, sleep, and other self-care rituals that restore you. Protect your energy so you have reserves left to uplift your child with positivity. Model healthy coping strategies and communicate that everyone experiences hard times. Show self-compassion instead of burning out. Seek help when needed because strengthening your ability to bounce back enables you to fully spread that empowerment to others.

Turn to supportive friends, a therapist, or rejuvenating activities. Model self-care strategies together. Show your child firsthand how to be resilient, while also making space to recharge when needed. Internal resilience allows both you and your child to weather life's inevitable challenges on the path toward building confidence. Remind yourself that setbacks are temporary, not a reflection of failure. Learn from other parents facing similar struggles with shy children. Be transparent about needing to recharge so your child understands that it's healthy and necessary.

Problem-Solving and Coping Strategies

Life will continue testing your shy child's confidence and self-esteem long after closing this book. Equip them with problem-solving and coping strategies to manage difficulties independently. When they face setbacks, anxiety, criticism, or discouragement, avoid immediately rushing in to rescue them. First, give them space to tap their inner strength and reflect on what they can do next. Ask prompts like "What ideas do you have?" and "What has worked in the past?" rather than solving the issue for them. Start by having them identify challenges where they can take ownership of the solution. Praise them for ideation and decision-making, not just positive outcomes. Remain patient as they self-reflect and think about what they can do differently, which will better equip them for independence.

Teach a step-by-step problem-solving process such as:

1. Defining the problem
2. Brainstorming solutions
3. Evaluating options
4. Implementing a plan
5. Reviewing what worked and didn't work

Model applying this process aloud through your own challenges. Have them practice with hypothetical scenarios. Over time, your child will gain the tools to constructively work through problems as they arise. Break bigger problems into smaller parts to make finding the solution less overwhelming. Use visual aids like flow charts and diagrams to reinforce the process. Frequently revisit and practice the technique so it becomes second nature over time.

Provide coping strategy suggestions such as:

- Taking deep breaths
- Journaling worries
- Exercising
- Creating art when overwhelmed

Also, give space for them to identify what self-soothing tactics help them feel centered and empowered. The ultimate goal is for your child to know how to manage their anxiety, reframe how they are feeling, and tap into inner resilience even when you're not there coaching them through it. Confidence comes from within, but the problem-solving and coping tools you instill in your child will help the confidence shine through. Experiment together with different coping strategies to discover their preferences. Set reminders to regularly practice these skills even on good days. Celebrate when you spot them independently employing helpful coping tactics.

When to Ask for Professional Help

The advice and strategies in this book aim to equip parents with tools to support their shy, insecure child in building confidence and self-esteem. However, some children require more help addressing issues deeper than everyday shyness. Pay attention to ongoing patterns like chronic anxiety, intense meltdowns, refusal to participate in school or activities, self-isolation, self-harm statements, or other mood changes that are impacting their quality of life. If your gut tells you something feels off, trust those instincts. Document any worrying behavioral changes to identify when they began escalating. Don't downplay red flags assuming it's just a phase—early intervention can help mitigate long-term impacts.

While it's natural for confidence levels to fluctuate, seek professional support if your child's emotional state prevents them from functioning normally at school, home, or socially for an extended time. The earlier you intervene with counseling, the sooner your child can learn healthy coping strategies, reframe unhelpful thoughts, and feel empowered again. Check if your health insurance or local health surgeries cover mental health services for early screening and access to care.

Finding the right form of help allows children struggling with crippling shyness or anxiety issues to thrive again. Counseling, therapy, support groups, life coaching, and mentoring can all provide external guidance during difficult times. Contact your pediatrician, school counselor, or local mental health organizations to explore options. Be an advocate for getting your child the support that they need. Prepare your child for the first appointment by explaining it's simply a conversation with someone who can help them understand and who is trained to help kids feel better.

With professional help, in addition to practicing the strategies in this book, your child can get back on track developing lifelong confidence and self-esteem. Our children's emotional well-being and ability to bounce back from adversity depend greatly on the mental health resources we provide. You've got this! Supports exist to help when challenges feel beyond your scope as a parent. Use your intuition, insight, and observation to determine when added support could benefit your shy child.

The Power of Peer Support Networks

In addition to parental support at home, peer communities can provide shy and insecure children with a powerful sense of belonging, normalcy, and courage to take risks. There is comfort in knowing others are going through the same struggles. Support groups, mentoring programs, clubs, and other networks replace isolation with solidarity.

Seek out school or community groups for shy, anxious, or introverted children led by trained moderators covering topics like friendship, self-esteem, managing emotions, trying new things, and overcoming fear. If none exist locally, explore online options making sure safety protocols are in place.

Connect with parents running social skills groups or clubs where children practice building confidence together through exercises such as asking questions in class, initiating play at recess, interviewing each other, and supporting shy peers. Structured activities in comforting atmospheres with families facing similar journeys can reduce the feelings of loneliness for both you and your child.

At school, encourage your child to start joining groups that focus on how children who are shy or low in confidence. Then, celebrate this! Explore teaming them up through cross-age mentorship with older students who've overcome shyness to help guide younger ones. Student-led initiatives give peers the opportunity to use their personal experiences to help. This confirms to your shy child that they are not alone and that parents and teachers recognize this.

Peer communities allow shy kids to give and receive compassion by relating to shared struggles firsthand from classmates navigating the same complex emotions. Bonds form with other kids as they realize that they aren't so different after all. What once seemed like an individual and lonely problem for your child transforms into a source of peer support and strength. Together, confidence can grow.

Cultivating Confidence Through Interests

While direct social skill-building is crucial, sometimes the best way to nurture self-assurance indirectly is by tapping into children's passionate interests. Pursuing natural talents and curiosities can relieve your shy child from feeling external performance pressures as they might shine in developing or just enjoying a skill that they love. Interests cultivate confidence organically.

Discover Innate Fascinations

Tune in to where your child's delight lies by assessing what books, web searches, drawings, or playtime themes captivate them. Does fantasy storytelling, building video game worlds, caring for creatures, coding programs, or tinkering with engineering ignite their inner spark? Follow their independent curiosity and questions to uncover what they are passionate about.

Help Broaden Exposure

If finances allow, provide equipment, classes, and memberships that they can use to explore potential interests that they didn't know were out there! This might also unlock confidence in things that they didn't previously think about or know about themselves. Surprise them with diverse magazines, museum visits, classes, tools, and project ideas surrounding topics that seem intriguing. Guide them in discovering new interests, whilst ensuring that they don't feel any pressure as they are exploring new things.

Encourage Skill Development

Help children understand that they shouldn't abandon new hobbies quickly but should give them some time to practice and get better. Discuss the benefits of how practice helps them improve and increase confidence. Frame progress as small steps and let them know that they shouldn't compare themselves with others. Break intimidating skills into incremental baby steps like basic sewing stitches before making full stuffed animals. Praise small acts of bravery when they try new challenges outside of their comfort zones. Share stories of your own experience in learning new skills and hobbies throughout your life.

Facilitate Idea Expression

Ensure that you have many supplies around the home that are tailored to your child's interests. Where finances allow, stock up on art media, musical instruments, gardening tools, robotics kits, or cameras to give your child the freedom to build their confidence through self-play. Quiet independent creativity will build your child's confidence and resilience.

Find Community Belonging

Help connect children to activities and mentors that share and promote the same interests such as clubs, conferences, online forums, and summer courses. Bonding over common passions stretches your child's social comfort faster through having a shared interest that they are already comfortable and confident discussing. Share your own experience of how you are encouraged by shared interests with your peers where you can demonstrate your abilities, for example, swimming, sewing club, card games, etc.

Spotlight Success

Find opportunities for your child to showcase their interests publicly but where there will be a minimum opportunity for negative feedback that could derail them, such as talent shows, contests, and open mic events. Manage their expectations and anxiety ahead of time, allowing them to choose what they are comfortable with, but encouraging them to stretch their comfort zones. Celebrate all courage, from backstage tech support to center stage.

What first appears as informal, personal amusement in some activities can become recognized over time as domain knowledge commanding respect and purpose. Nurturing your child's interests and encouraging them to try new things that spark an interest illuminates undiscovered strengths and changes how they perceive themselves. Their confidence reflects talents feeling a unique match.

Case Study: Evan

Evan is a shy 11-year-old who avoids social risks and gets extremely nervous speaking to unfamiliar people. Transitioning to middle school overwhelmed Evan, between bigger classes, trying out for sports teams, and maintaining old friendships. He began skipping events and retreating to isolation out of fear.

Seeing their normally vibrant son withdraw, Evan's parents compassionately discussed concerns without judgment. Together, they brainstormed small social goals that felt manageable, such as joining one extracurricular club. Evan chose the coding club, given his secret interest in programming and the smaller group size.

He felt anxiety in the first few meetings, but Evan persisted with encouragement. His parents modeled coping strategies when he was frustrated, such as taking calming breaks. Evan discovered peers who shared gaming interests which in turn made it easier for him to make social connections. After Evan considered quitting, his parents reminded him that each effort makes interactions easier over time.

Bit by bit, Evan expanded his comfort zone by trying new projects, making online gaming friends, and pushing through when he felt nervous presenting at competitions. Bumps happened, but focusing on self-improvement goals kept Evan motivated. Recently, he proudly led his team in debugging a challenging sequence of code.

Evan's parents trust that he's gaining lifelong confidence and resilience through these strategies that allow him to practice social interactions bit by bit. They keep lines of communication open with Evan so the support that they give can be adjusted when needed, and they demonstrate how to give healthy responses to setbacks that he may have. Evan's inner strength is what will sustain him through life's inevitable obstacles. His family believes in that power within him.

Case Study: Anna

Anna is a bright 9-year-old who has always been incredibly shy and anxious in social situations. She has trouble raising her hand in class and making friends. Anna's mom, Claire, has tried various strategies from praise and encouragement to exposure therapy, but Anna continued to isolate herself, avoid risks, and struggle with low self-confidence.

After another rough first week of fourth grade, Claire decided it was time to seek professional support. She talked with Anna's pediatrician, who recommended both counseling and an evaluation from the school psychologist.

The counseling provided Anna with a safe space to open up about her fears of judgment and failure. Over time, Anna learned coping techniques to manage anxiety. The psychologist evaluated Anna for any learning challenges and recommended that she join a social skills group.

At the same time, Claire continued reinforcing a growth mindset, problem-solving skills, and resilience at home with Anna. She struck an intentional balance of emotional support while still gently pushing Anna out of her comfort zone. After a shaky start, Claire also showed how important self-care is, including taking the girls for special mother-daughter days each month.

While slow, steady progress isn't always easy, Anna is undeniably growing in confidence. Recently she volunteered to help new students transition into her school. Claire still watches for signs that her daughter feels truly overwhelmed, but she trusts in the professional team supporting Anna alongside the unconditional love at home. She reminds herself every child travels their path at their own pace when blossoming into the strong, self-assured person they're meant to become.

Opportunities for Practice

The path of nurturing confidence and self-belief in a shy child has its fair share of obstacles. When faced with setbacks, anxiety, criticism, or other adversities, remind your child that challenges are merely opportunities to practice resilience. Avoid immediately rescuing them from discomfort. First, give them space to tap into their inner problem-solving strengths. Over time, also demonstrate your own healthy responses to life's inevitable difficulties. Whether through positive self-talk, seeking help, or centering strategies, teach coping mechanisms aligned with your child's interests. Check in on their emotional state without judgment so you can give them additional support where needed. Your unconditional love provides your child with the security for them to explore all the different ways to build their confidence independently and safely. By equipping children to self-soothe and bounce back after stumbles, you give them the greatest gift of believing wholly in themselves.

Conclusion

As parents, our deepest hope is to raise happy, confident children equipped to build fulfilling connections and reach their full potential. Yet for those shy, hesitant children who struggle socially, that vision can feel out of reach. The distress that we notice when they avoid playground games, new friends, speaking up at school, or trying new things poses risks to their safety, growth, and future success is something that we desperately want to help them manage.

Equipping our sensitive children to confidently navigate the emotional intricacies of childhood friendships, find their voice amidst their peers, take academic risks, and develop resilience against exclusion and criticism is important and can't wait. These signs in their behavior show us that they need our help and intervention in compassionately supporting and putting in place strategies for them to manage this.

The knowledge provided across these chapters aims to alleviate parents' and caregivers' worries about how we can support our shy children by providing guidance through proven strategies. With insight into accurate definitions, developmental impacts, recognizable symptoms, supportive environments, and targeted skill-building strategies, you now have a comprehensive tool kit to help your child manage this and grow in confidence.

While shyness may not fully disappear, it can absolutely loosen the grip on how disabling it might feel for a shy child in social situations. By setting examples ourselves, putting in place strategies and guidelines to help children understand and accept themselves, and seeking professional support when needed, we provide our children with the best chance to live a full life. Most importantly, the combination of giving our children unconditional love and support, irrespective of where they are on the shyness spectrum, and at the same time encouraging them to push the boundaries of their growing confidence gives them the self-belief in themselves. Confidence was always innately residing inside them, anxiously awaiting being unlocked. Our approach by leveraging the different strategies in this book, hands them the keys to unlock that confidence!

If there are times when you doubt your ability to help your child progress and grow in confidence, always remember the incredible capacity and resilience all children have inside them to evolve and progress when surrounded by patience and care. Your commitment to understanding and nurturing your child's path with compassion, and not judgment, has enabled them to grow in confidence and potentially use their emotional sensitivity to help better our society. It's never too late to support a shy child in realizing their inner confidence to make and maintain the relationships and connections that they make through life. This book provided a road map and some strategies to support that, and in their own time, your shy child will soon develop self-confidence and self-belief to thrive.

References

Asendorpf, J. B. (2008). Living up to our expectations and beyond: Commentary on Kenrick & Funder (1988). *Perspectives on Psychological Science,* 3(1), 75-76.

Clauss, J. A., & Blackford, J. U. (2014). Neural correlates of shyness and their relations to social anxiety in schizophrenia. *Schizophrenia Research,* 154(0 1–3), 27–33. https://doi.org/10.1016/j.schres.2014.01.023

Crozier, W. R. (2014). Differentiating shyness and embarrassment. V. Zayas & C. Hazan (Eds.), *Bases of adult attachment: Linking brain, mind and behavior* (pp. 61-76). Springer.

Eggum, N. D., et al. (2011). Emotion understanding, theory of mind, and prosocial orientation: Relations over time in early childhood. *The Journal of Positive Psychology,* 6(1), 4-16.

La Greca, A. M., & Lopez, N. (1998). Social anxiety among adolescents: Linkages with peer relations and friendships. *Journal of Abnormal Child Psychology,* 26(2), 83-94.

LoParo, D., & Waldman, I. D. (2014). Twin studies, molecular genetics, and shyness. R. J. Coplan & J. Bowker (Eds.), *A handbook of solitude: Psychological perspectives on social isolation, social withdrawal, and being alone* (pp. 314–336). Wiley Blackwell.

Gifford-Smith, M.E. & Brownell, C.A. (2003). Childhood peer relationships: Social acceptance, friendships, and peer networks. *Journal of School Psychology,* 41(4), 235-284.

Jones, D.E. & Gordon, E.M. (2016). The relation between childhood shyness and adolescent anxiety disorders in the clinical setting. *Clinical Pediatrics,* 55(1), 9-12.

Harris, K.R. (2018). Educational implications of associations between children's peer risk for exclusion and academic risk status. *Exceptional Children,* 84(3), 280-297.

Smith, A. & Watson, B. (2019). The significance of childhood friendships for adult health and wellbeing. *American Journal of Public Health,* 109(3), 444-446.

Renshaw, P.D. & Arslan, G. (2016). Psychological, social, and cognitive correlates of adolescent life skill development. *Journal of Human Behavior in the Social Environment,* 26(7), 646-660.

A NOTE FROM THE

AUTHOR

I do hope you have enjoyed reading this fascinating book as much as I enjoyed researching and writing it. We also have a companion workbook available (Build Your Shy Kid's Self-Confidence Workbook), that can be used for you to track your actions, observations and progress in supporting your shy child in increasing their confidence.

Just scan the QR code below and it will take you to the link!

Scan me!

I have spent a long time researching and writing this book for you, the reader, and if the book was of interest and enjoyable for you to read, I would respectfully request that you leave a positive review. This will support me in getting my book to a wider audience.

Thank you for reading.

Printed in Great Britain
by Amazon